I lost someone very dear to me as I was reading this book, and Dena's words were a balm to my grieving heart. Although this is the story of her own deeply personal journey through loss, the way she so honestly shares her thoughts and feelings, along with the carefully chosen Scripture passages and her wise reflections through it all, made me feel not so alone in my own grief process. Dena beautifully weaves together her journey through grief and her travels through Scotland in a way that is both greatly helpful and deeply hopeful. This book is more than a mere memoir, it is a kind companion on the road through pain and loss, gently taking your hand and reminding you to lift your eyes and look for the Light.

JENNIFER TUCKER,
best-selling author of Breath as Prayer, Present in Prayer, & Prayer in Motion

This book feels like being gently accompanied through grief. With honesty and grace, Dena shares her journey of loss, remembrance, and healing, interlacing the beauty of Scotland, the depth of the psalms, and the ache of saying goodbye to her beloved parents. For anyone walking through the long aftermath of loss, these pages offer comfort, companionship, and hope.

NIKKI COLLINS,
National Coordinator, 1001 New Worshiping Communities Presbyterian Church (USA).

When Anxiety Strikes

When Anxiety Strikes is an excellent book for anxiety management and a valuable resource within the Christian tradition. We are fortunate to have this book combining personal narrative, pastoral wisdom, and clinical insights.

Harold G, Koenig, MD
director of the Center for Spirituality, Theology, and Health, Duke University Medical Center

Anxiety is running rampant not just in our culture, but in this moment in history. The Hobbes offer a down-to-earth, practical approach to overcoming anxiety that everyone can benefit from.

Margaret Feinberg,
author of The God You Need to Know

LIFT UP YOUR EYES

Thirty Days through Psalms, Scotland, and Grief

DENA DOUGLAS HOBBS

ISBN-13: 979-8-9947618-0-9

Printed in the United States of America First Edition

To Mom and Dad.

I love you. I miss you.

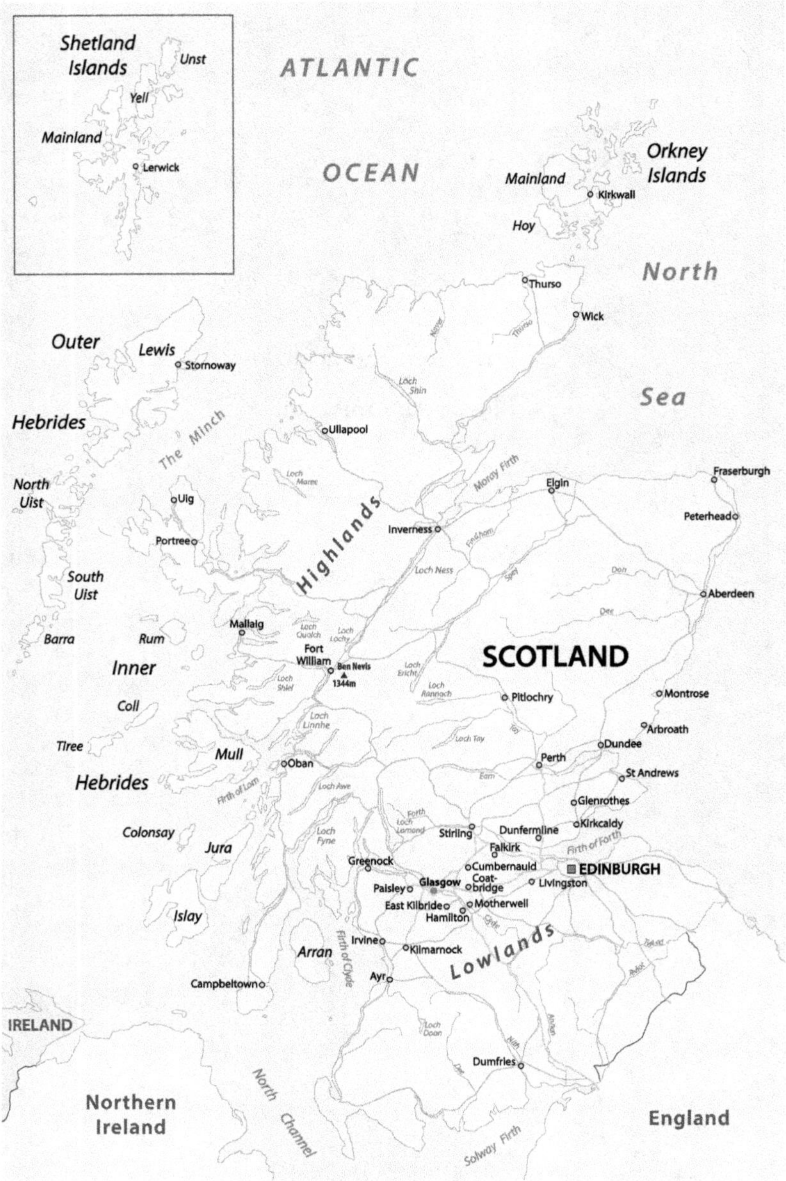
Shetland Islands
Unst
Yell
Mainland
Lerwick
ATLANTIC
OCEAN
Orkney Islands
Mainland
Kirkwall
Hoy
North
Sea
Thurso
Wick
Outer
Hebrides
Lewis
Stornoway
Loch Shin
Ullapool
The Minch
Loch Maree
North Uist
Uig
Portree
South Uist
Barra
Rum
Inner
Hebrides
Coll
Tiree
Mull
Colonsay
Jura
Islay
Arran
Moray Firth
Elgin
Fraserburgh
Peterhead
Inverness
Highlands
Loch Ness
Aberdeen
Mallaig
Loch Quoich
Loch Lochy
Fort William
Ben Nevis
1344m
Loch Shiel
Loch Ericht
Loch Rannoch
SCOTLAND
Pitlochry
Montrose
Arbroath
Loch Linnhe
Loch Tay
Dundee
Perth
Oban
St Andrews
Firth of Lorn
Loch Awe
Glenrothes
Kirkcaldy
Loch Lomond
Stirling
Dunfermline
Loch Fyne
Falkirk
Firth of Forth
Greenock
Cumbernauld
EDINBURGH
Glasgow
Paisley
Coat-bridge
Livingston
East Kilbride
Motherwell
Hamilton
Irvine
Kilmarnock
Lowlands
Firth of Clyde
Ayr
Campbeltown
IRELAND
Loch Doon
Dumfries
Northern Ireland
North Channel
Solway Firth
England

INTRODUCTION

I NEVER PLANNED to write this book. Moreover, I never planned to get sucker punched by grief so hard that I could not breathe. But if you are reading these words, you probably understand. So let me start by saying I'm sorry. I'm sorry for whoever and whatever you lost that caused you to pick up this book.

For me it was my parents. My eighty-five year old mother died unexpectedly, with my ninety-year old father dying three months later. My dad had been declining for years with dementia. But it goes like that sometimes. You lose one and the other follows.

I thought I would be okay. They had lived long, full lives. I thought I was ready. But I was not ready for the deep sadness, exhaustion, anger, and confusion that rolled over me like waves. Also, I couldn't write. Putting words on paper is how I make sense of life. For whatever reason, there was silence for a while.

A year after dad died, my family took a trip to Scotland to visit the land of my paternal ancestors. I wanted to close out my year of grief celebrating the people who made me. It was a deeply moving trip in many ways. And when I came home the words started flowing like a Scottish stream. They eventually flowed into this book.

I offer my thoughts and reflections to you now with

a prayer. I pray they bring you light, comfort, and hope. I pray they help you know you are not alone in your sadness and anger. I pray they help you find strength and healing through your faith.

I invite you to read these words slowly. Let them steep inside you like a strong cup of tea. It took me quite a while to write them all. So no rush reading. The idea is to read a chapter a day for thirty days. But feel free to take as long as you like.

Some chapters may bring back hard memories or stir up strong emotions. I wish I could include a lace bordered handkerchief so you know it is okay to cry. I hope you laugh some too. I encourage you to keep a journal handy so you can write your own words that help you process your grief. It certainly helped me.

And I hope you like the Psalms. Even if you only read the Psalms each day, you will find sweet balm. These wonderful songs of heartache and longing, frustration and faith. May they give you permission to feel all your feelings and then let them rest in the lap of God.

Now, friends, Beannachd Dia dhuit. The blessings of God be with you as you read. I am praying for you.—Dena

CHAPTER 1

PSALM 27:1–9, 13–14

1 The LORD is my light and my salvation;
whom shall I fear?
The LORD is the stronghold of my life;
of whom shall I be afraid?

2 When evildoers assail me
to devour my flesh—
my adversaries and foes—
they shall stumble and fall.

3 Though an army encamp against me,
my heart shall not fear;
though war rise up against me,
yet I will be confident.

4 One thing I asked of the LORD;
this I seek:
to live in the house of the LORD
all the days of my life,
to behold the beauty of the LORD,
and to inquire in his temple.

5 For he will hide me in his shelter
in the day of trouble;
he will conceal me under the cover of his tent;
he will set me high on a rock.

6 Now my head is lifted up
above my enemies all around me,
and I will offer in his tent
sacrifices with shouts of joy;
I will sing and make melody to the LORD.

7 Hear, O LORD when I cry aloud;
be gracious to me and answer me!
8 "Come," my heart says, "seek his face!"
Your face, LORD, do I seek.
9 Do not hide your face from me.

13 I believe that I shall see the goodness of the LORD
in the land of the living.
14 Wait for the LORD;
be strong, and let your heart take courage;
wait for the LORD!

GLASGOW

OUR PLANE DESCENDS through thick grey clouds. The air is as dreary as the past year of my life. I see patches of morning light shining down on one green field after another. I can hardly believe I am finally seeing Scotland with my own eyes. My husband, Jason, leans over to look out the airplane window with me. "Are you ready for this?" he asks as he gives my arm a squeeze.

"I think so," I give him a tentative smile. "Ready or not, here Glasgow comes!" Honestly, I have been waiting for this moment most of my life. My dad always talked about how we Douglases came from Scotland. He would spend free moments researching our genealogy and tracing the family line back to the lowlands outside Glasgow. He loved wearing his Douglas tartan tie. He would put it on at Christmastime and give a wide smile.

Scotland became part of what my dad was made of. And he passed that connection to Caledonia right down to me as well. So when Dad started dying, I knew I needed to see this land that made us both. I needed to go to the land of our ancestors to help lay him to rest.

I needed some space to grieve. Losing my parents three months apart was not something I was prepared for. Who could be? We had spent years saying goodbye to Dad as dementia slowly took him from us. And then Mom's health began to fail as well. As much as our family scrambled to care for both of them, my mom's decline stayed one step ahead. In the end, she went quickly, leaving us to take care of her husband of over 60 years.

Dad was lost without her. I was lost without her. But instead of grieving Mom, I spent all my energy taking care of Dad. We hired sitters and researched memory care units. I stopped by every afternoon to hold Dad's hand and dry his tears. It was excruciating.

When it became clear Dad would quickly follow Mom in death, I began imagining life without them. I was glad my father's suffering would soon be at an end, but also bereft. How could I say goodbye to two parents in one year? How could I hold all this sadness?

I knew I would need to take such loss seriously. I gave myself "a year of grief" to lay low and recover. I did not yet know what that year would ask of me, but I anticipated it would be challenging. So, I started planning a trip to Scotland to help me process my thoughts and find motivation to start my new life without them. I needed to see the goodness of the Lord in the land of the living again. I needed hope to shine a light into my fog of sadness. This longing was at the heart of my journey—the ache under all the planning.

I was fortunate not to grieve alone. Jason and our two young adult children, Eli and Libby, were right beside me—in the loss, in the grieving, and on our trip to Caledonia, the land of the Scots.

And of course, I had my faith. As much as I questioned the hard circumstances of my parents' deaths, I never questioned the love of God. In their dying and my grieving, I kept asking God to hold me in the storm, and God was faithful—not by lifting me out of it, but by walking through it with me. Even when I had more questions than answers, I knew God was holding my hand and walking alongside me on this hard path.

The flight attendant comes over the speaker and reminds us to put our tray tables up and lift our seats to their upright position. Not loving the turbulence of the landing, I close my eyes, grip the arms of my seat, and pray the opening lines of Psalm 27. "The LORD is my light and my salvation, whom shall I fear? The LORD is the stronghold of my life, of whom shall I be afraid?" My shaking hands begin to still from my fear of turbulence and my quaking heart eases from worry about facing my grief head on.

Whatever lies ahead on this two-week trip, I know God will be on the road before us, making a way for us. Whatever lies before me in life after my parents' death, I know I will not face it alone. As the plane lands, I summon my courage to step into the path before me—trusting that same God who is my light will also be my strength, come what may.

CHAPTER 2

PSALM 1

1 Happy are those
who do not follow the advice of the wicked
or take the path that sinners tread
or sit in the seat of scoffers,
2 but their delight is in the law of the LORD,
and on his law they meditate day and night.

3 They are like trees
planted by streams of water,
which yield their fruit in its season,
and their leaves do not wither.
In all that they do, they prosper.

4 The wicked are not so
but are like chaff that the wind drives away.
5 Therefore the wicked will not stand in the judgment
nor sinners in the congregation of the righteous,
6 for the LORD watches over the way of the righteous,
but the way of the wicked will perish.

NECROPOLIS

"HOW MUCH FARTHER?" I ask, climbing another hill. It seems we are climbing to the very summit of Glasgow. Jason looks back from his position as point person. "About half a mile. Almost there."

When the pub server recommended we visit the city's Necropolis, we neglected to ask exactly how far away it was or how much of the walk was uphill. "What is a necropolis anyway?" asks my son Eli, from his position behind his dad.

"Necro means dead, and polis means city. The city of the dead. It is a cemetery." I may be the slowest walker and last in our line on the city sidewalk, but I do remember my Latin and Greek. I have also spent a fair amount of time walking among the dead this past year, so the name resonates.

My daughter Libby takes off her camera's lens cap to catch a quick shot of an alley we pass. "It's pretty though, right? The woman said it would be a great place for me to photograph."

"Well, we will soon find out," Jason responds. "We are almost there." When I look up, I can see the church steeple peeking out above the leafy trees. We are soon in the cathedral's courtyard, staring in awe at the ancient stone building before us. We mix in with the tourist groups as we walk through the huge wooden doors.

"Let's go this way," says Libby as we peel off to walk along the left side of the church. The smell of old stone and incense fills the air. "What are all these plaques for?" She points to the engraved stone slabs on the floor.

I sigh before I tell her. Neither she nor I love thinking about the bones of dead people. It hits too close these days. "Well, they used to bury important people below the floor of the church. Those are their grave markers," I respond. Libby gives me a wary look as she adjusts her camera for the dimly lit interior and snaps a shot.

After half an hour of marveling at the stained glass and stonework of the sanctuary, we make our way outside. "I think this is the path to the cemetery." Jason, as always, leads our way. We wind our way above the church towards the steel-grey clouds hanging in the sky. As we walk over the Bridge of Sighs, all we see around us are grave markers. Some are simple, and some are better classed as monuments. Below us, the rain-washed city stretches out for miles.

I marvel at how Glasgow has placed a cemetery at the top of this high hill. Most cities put a castle or fortress at the highest elevations. But here, they put the cemetery in pride of place. To me, it shows something about what the 19th-century Glaswegians valued. Even above the church, they honored their dead.

I take a deep breath as I turn another switchback in the cemetery, climbing up into a cloud of fog. I could learn a lesson. I have struggled with visiting my own parents' graves this past year. I don't know if it is because the mausoleum they lie in is so cold and sterile or because I don't want to face the pain of my grief, but I resist visiting their final resting place.

I resist a lot of things.

Often, I wish I was doing better than I am. I wish I were as fine as I tell everyone else I am. Is it because I think I must? Modern American society, after all, has given up most of our grieving rituals. We don't wear black anymore or opt out of parties. I felt pressure after a few months to leave my dead behind and go on with my life as usual.

But things aren't as usual. There is a gaping hole of silence where my parents used to be, and I don't know how to make sense of it all. I do try to keep reminders of them close by. Immediately after my mom passed, I packed up her makeup bag and brought it home with me. I have worn different shades of her signature peach lipstick for over a year. I wear one of my dad's old shirts regularly and gravitate toward our shared favorite foods.

Mostly, I try to live in a way that they would be happy with—to make them proud. Can parents be proud after they die? My heart earnestly hopes they can.

I look up to the towering statue of John Knox, the great reformer of a wounded church, wondering if he has an answer for me. But he is silent. All I hear is the wind whipping around my ears.

As my daughter takes photos of the statue reflected in a nearby puddle, I think about the legacy of these hardworking, God-loving Scots. Surely they had their share of grief and loss as well. Did their grief send them into a midlife crisis also? I can't imagine their lives afforded them such luxury.

I think of the stories I know of my immediate ancestors. My Grandaddy was one of many siblings born to his parents in the woods of Tennessee. I remember how he worked so hard all his life, first logging, then working at the cement plant, and finally repairing military airplanes. Even when he was in his nineties and the only sibling left on this earth, he kept busy planting a garden and keeping us all supplied with fresh vegetables year-round. Though he didn't go to church much, Grandaddy seemed to understand the wisdom of Psalm 1—the one who delights in the law of the LORD is like a tree planted by streams of water, giving fruit in its season.

How many days did I help Grandaddy pick the fruits of his garden? He never complained about missing his family, which he surely did. He just kept his head down and tried to make something useful of his time left on earth. If only I could stay as rooted as he was.

And then there was my grandmother, who outlived not only her siblings but also her husband and one son. She was more vocal about her grief, but she tried her best not to get stuck in it. Even on the hardest days, she would make a meal or prune her roses. Though she was not perfect by any means—who among us is—she tried to do what she could to add something good to the world and to alleviate the suffering of others, often by making a meal or giving a little something to us kids.

I wonder if she knew how much we would miss her when she was gone, this last link to a generation of ancestors. She seemed to have some sense of the hole that would be left. She spent her last years handing down heirlooms and telling us stories one more time, as if crocheted blankets could root us to our heritage of hard-working people who try to love God and do the right thing. Not only do these items root me now, they wrap me in the comfort of her love.

Though I will never be able to garden like my Grandaddy, crochet like Great-Grandmother Douglas, or cook like Grandma, I can do what I can: keep planting myself in God's Word, loving my Creator and those around me. I can send cards to the sick like my mom did and tell Dad's favorite jokes to bring a laugh. I can try to make the world a little brighter, even on the dreary days.

As we get ready to head back down the rain-slicked hill, I silently salute those buried here one more time. The lives of the dead matter. The impact they made on our world matters. I straighten my back and lift my head, determined to live my life in a way that will matter. I will bear whatever fruit I can into this hungry world. Will Grandaddy be proud? One day, I will know. Until then, I resolutely keep my eyes turned to the LORD.

CHAPTER 3

PSALM 102:1–11, 18–28

1 Hear my prayer, O LORD;
let my cry come to you.
2 Do not hide your face from me
in the day of my distress.
Incline your ear to me;
answer me speedily in the day when I call.

3 For my days pass away like smoke,
and my bones burn like a furnace.
4 My heart is stricken and withered like grass;
I am too wasted to eat my bread.
5 Because of my loud groaning,
my bones cling to my skin.
6 I am like a desert owl of the wilderness,
like a little owl of the waste places.
7 I lie awake;

I am like a lonely bird on the housetop.
8 All day long my enemies taunt me;
those who deride me use my name for a curse.
9 Indeed, I eat ashes like bread
and mingle tears with my drink,

10 because of your indignation and anger,
for you have lifted me up and thrown me aside.
11 My days are like a lengthening shadow;
I wither away like grass.

18 Let this be recorded for a generation to come,
so that a people yet unborn may praise the Lord:
19 that he looked down from his holy height,
from heaven the LORD looked at the earth,
20 to hear the groans of the prisoners,
to set free those who were doomed to die,
21 so that the name of the LORD
may be declared in Zion
and his praise in Jerusalem,
22 when peoples gather together,
and kingdoms, to serve the LORD.

23 He has broken my strength in midcourse;
he has shortened my days.
24 "O my God," I say, "do not take me away
at the midpoint of my life,
you whose years endure
throughout all generations."

25 Long ago you laid the foundation of the earth,
and the heavens are the work of your hands.
26 They will perish, but you endure;
they will all wear out like a garment.
You change them like clothing, and they pass away,
27 but you are the same, and your years have no end.
28 The children of your servants shall live secure;
their offspring shall be established in your presence.

TRAINS

WE FOLLOW JASON through a door off a street in Glasgow. We know our hotel is nearby, but we just can't figure out where. Suddenly, I realize we have entered a train station. In fact, we have entered Glasgow Central Station.

Pretty soon, we're walking in a line along the train platforms, trailing our luggage behind us. I don't even care about the hotel anymore. I have always loved trains and train stations. A fact inversely proportional to how often I get to actually ride them. The wind from a passing train blows my hair into my face. As I move it away from my eyes, a dream opens up before me.

Past the rush of the departing trains is a line of shops, quaint and unmistakably Scottish with their dark wood and stone exteriors. I feel like I have dropped into a movie. "Mom, it's like Harry Potter!" my daughter cries, skipping ahead for a better view. As we walk beneath the large analog clock suspended from the ceiling, we spot the entrance to our hotel nestled at the end of the shops. My smile makes my face ache. My muscles aren't used to smiling this wide.

After we check in, Jason and I walk down to the bar for

tea and a snack. We will venture out for Indian food later, but for now our hungry bodies still think it's lunchtime in Georgia and demand sustenance. As I munch my short-bread, I stare out the window overlooking the train station. My eyes can't get enough of the people arriving and leaving. I keep watching to see when the next train will depart.

There is something so comforting about the schedule of trains. Even if they are a little late, you know they will eventually arrive. And as soon as one train arrives, another will depart. It is kind of like watching the ebb and flow of ocean waves, but with people. The predictable rhythm of trains has been the background music of my life, having lived a mile from a train track for the past twenty-five years. Their regularity is an anchor when life gets chaotic.

The sound and rhythm of them soothes me. Coming and going. Always coming and going.

There is something deeply true about this rhythm. Nothing stays forever. Certainly not people. As the Psalmist says, our days pass away like smoke, and we wither and fade like grass. But even as one person is swept away by the wind, another generation will sprout from the earth. Coming and Going. We are always coming and going.

There seems to be a phenomenon in families where new babies are born near the time that elders die. I don't know if the impending new life gives the elder permission to let go of life, or if the leaving of an elder creates a void for new life to fill.

With our family, it was somewhere in the middle. When my niece and her toddler came to say goodbye to Mom, my niece was only a few weeks pregnant with another child. None of us knew. I am not even sure if she knew. But a little less than nine months after my mother passed away, a great-granddaughter was born and given Mom's name as a middle name.

Life goes and life comes.

One person fades away while another one springs to life.

Psalm 102 reminds us that we are impermanent—and that each season in our life and life as a whole—only lasts so long. We are born, and that life has its season. Then, in our old age, or middle age, or even youth, comes the time to die. People telling me it was my mom's time to die, the end of her season, never brings me comfort. Who gets to decide how much time is enough?

But somehow, the knowledge that the overarching force of life goes on soothes. Though my parents are not physically with me anymore, their legacy remains. In me and my brother, our children, and our children's children. Though their physical absence feels like the end of my world some days, life itself goes on. The grass withers and dies, then new seeds sprout in the spring. Nothing lasts forever except God, who laid the foundations of the earth and created us all by hand.

There is something about this web of life, its strings woven together by the Great Creator who holds me. I am sad now. But one day I will laugh again. I feel broken down now, but one day I will be rebuilt. I am silent now, but one day words will flow again.

When Mom passed, our family took a hit, then it grew again in numbers and in joy. Who knows how many great-grandchildren Mom will end up with one day? Who knows what her legacy will be?

In the same way, my grief won't be forever. I have taken

a big hit. But who knows what plans God has to grow my life again?

I don't know how many days are left in my life. We do not get to know how long our train ride will last. I am only a passenger, not the conductor. I only know that one day, my own journey on this earth will be over. I will blow away like smoke. Some days this thought is painful, but today it comforts me. I am no better than anyone else. My wave will hit the shore and then recede back into the great ocean of God.

So what do we do with the days we have left? How do we spend our journey? I hope for days of laughing and building and growing in my future, even as I accept there will be more days of sorrow and pain and loss.

But today? Today I will eat and drink and be merry. Even as I ache for those who are not here. I will enjoy the gift of this moment in Glasgow with my family. I will let myself be filled with wonder and joy and give thanks for the gift of this day.

CHAPTER 4

PSALM 137

1 By the rivers of Babylon—
there we sat down, and there we wept
when we remembered Zion.
2 On the willows there
we hung up our harps.
3 For there our captors
asked us for songs,
and our tormentors asked for mirth, saying,
"Sing us one of the songs of Zion!"

4 How could we sing the LORD's song
in a foreign land?
5 If I forget you, O Jerusalem,
let my right hand wither!
6 Let my tongue cling to the roof of my mouth,
if I do not remember you,
if I do not set Jerusalem
above my highest joy.

7 Remember, O LORD, against the Edomites
the day of Jerusalem's fall,

how they said, "Tear it down! Tear it down!
Down to its foundations!"
8 O daughter Babylon, you devastator!
Happy shall they be who pay you back
what you have done to us!
9 Happy shall they be who take your little ones
and dash them against the rock!

EXILE

AS I WALK over to the verdant pasture, a lamb lifts his head to watch me. His white ears perk up to hear what I will do next. His mom, on the other hand, keeps munching the damp clover, unconcerned by my presence. I don't know exactly what I expected the Clan Douglas estate to be like, but public grounds complete with sheep pastures were not on my list. But I find myself glad of their gentle presence.

I have alternately been dreaming of and dreading this moment, this pilgrimage to my ancestral grounds. Ever since my dad entered hospice after the death of my mom, I knew I needed to stand in this spot and honor my ancestors. My homeless heart needed to find the home of our ancestors and see if any balm lay there. On the drive over from Glasgow, I bubbled up with grief and gratitude. Gratitude for Dad, Grandaddy, and all those forefathers who made me who I am today. And yet, so much grief at the loss of them.

Just two weeks ago I took a different pilgrimage. On the first anniversary of Dad's death, I drove across my own county to the place where he was born. Even though the spot lies only 20 minutes from my current home, I needed to go back in time to honor my Dad's beginnings, and therefore my own. Clinchfield, Georgia, isn't much to look at now, but decades ago it was a thriving plant town with its own company store and housing. Ninety years ago, in one of the cement plant houses, my dad took his first breath.

But that day, driving past field after field, I kept remembering when he took his last. The man on that deathbed was so different from the man who raised me. The strong man who would carry me on his shoulders with ease now faded before my eyes. Watching this once vital, capable man slowly lose his mental capacities and then his physical was the hardest ten years of my life. Losing him was so painful, I wanted to gain a piece of him back any way I could.

Enter the great Scotland pilgrimage. After an eight-hour flight and some fretful driving on the "wrong" side of the road, my family and I were finally in the county where my great-great-great-grandfather once lived. And somehow, looking out at the pastoral scene in front of me, I feel at home.

Partly, this is because my ancestors had sailed to the southeastern United States and stayed because it felt like home to them too. Because in some ways, it was. The rolling hills, small rivers, and gentle mountains of Southern Appalachia are quite similar to the Scottish lowlands. I am sure immigrants who had farmed in County Lanarkshire arrived in Appalachia and thought, "I can figure this out, I have farmed this land before." So they built a home and plowed a field.

But do I know what I am doing in County Lanarkshire?

I leave the green pastures full of sheep and walk toward

the pond. As my children photograph the many ducks, I stand and take in the scene. Looking at the rolling hills stretching out as far as the eye can see, I wonder how hard it must have been for my family to leave this beautiful place. How frightening it must have felt to give all this up and begin a strange new life.

But in some ways, I know that landscape too. I could never have imagined how uprooting it would be to say goodbye to both my parents within three months. After losing them, I felt exiled from my own life, a stranger to myself. Who even was I anymore? A grown adult who suddenly felt like an orphaned child.

But I, too, asked, like the Psalmist, "How can I sing the LORD's song in a strange land?" Like the Israelites, I wrestled with anger and confusion and total disorientation. But I knew I had to pick myself up from beside the strange river of grief and dry my tears. We can do nothing while in exile but build a new house and plow a new field. I wasn't quite ready to plant anything yet, but it was time to get a lay of this new land.

For even in a strange land, we know we are not alone. God goes with us, helping us make a new life in a strange place. And there are reminders of home. It strikes me as I turn back to the sheep that my own brother became a sheep farmer. Our ancestors must be laughing—you can take a Douglas out of Scotland, but 200 years later his descendant will still be raising sheep and caring for the land. I hope they know their legacy lives on in our lives.

As I dip my hand into the brown river that has run through this patch of land for centuries, I am comforted. For some things remain constant even through time and change. Not just these green pastures and cool waters of

Scotland, but the loving presence of God and the life God gifts each of us in love. My parents aren't truly gone. I can no longer call them and tell them about this wonderful trip, but they are with me. Their love rejoicing over me even as I reach out to them beyond the veil. And God's love surrounds us all.

I consider taking something with me from my ancestral grounds—a rock or a blade of grass. But I decide I don't need to, for this land is already inside me, and will always be with me. When I feel the exile of grief, I will call to mind these green pastures and refreshing waters and know that God, my shepherd, is with me, through the shadow of death and beyond.

CHAPTER 5

PSALM 51:1–12, 15–17

1 Have mercy on me, O God,
according to your steadfast love;
according to your abundant mercy,
blot out my transgressions.
2 Wash me thoroughly from my iniquity,
and cleanse me from my sin.

3 For I know my transgressions,
and my sin is ever before me.
4 Against you, you alone, have I sinned
and done what is evil in your sight,
so that you are justified in your sentence
and blameless when you pass judgment.
5 Indeed, I was born guilty,
a sinner when my mother conceived me.

6 You desire truth in the inward being;
therefore teach me wisdom in my secret heart.
7 Purge me with hyssop, and I shall be clean;
wash me, and I shall be whiter than snow.
8 Let me hear joy and gladness;

let the bones that you have crushed rejoice.
9 Hide your face from my sins,
and blot out all my iniquities.

10 Create in me a clean heart, O God,
and put a new and right spirit within me.
11 Do not cast me away from your presence,
and do not take your holy spirit from me.
12 Restore to me the joy of your salvation,
and sustain in me a willing spirit.

15 O LORD, open my lips,
and my mouth will declare your praise.
16 For you have no delight in sacrifice;
if I were to give a burnt offering,
you would not be pleased.
17 The sacrifice acceptable to God is a broken spirit;
a broken and contrite heart, O God, you will not despise.

SELF DESTRUCTION

AS I CLIMB the slope to what is left of the Douglas castle, I take in the lone tower on the hilltop. When I began researching my family's ancestral home, I learned the once-glorious castle that stood on the estate was in ruins. At first, I assumed the castle was destroyed in battle. The Douglases were, after all, strong supporters of Robert the Bruce and fought fiercely for Scottish freedom from the English.

The actual story is much more complex. A series of mansions rose here over the centuries. The last one, built in the 1800s, was destroyed not by battle but by mining in the 1930s. The disruption of neighboring ground rippled outward and made the earth beneath the historic mansion unstable. The house had to be torn down. Only an adjacent tower from the 17th-century castle once damaged by fire remained. The most striking part: the mining was organized by the Earl at the time, Charles Douglas-Home. The Douglases essentially destroyed their own homeplace. I felt that ruin in myself.

When I read the story of Castle Douglas' demise, I immediately thought, "That makes sense." For if I know anything about my relatives, it's that they are self-destructive. For years, the Douglases fought one another for control of the clan, then for high standing in Scottish politics—sometimes even getting themselves murdered by their "friends" who wanted power more. Even now, people argue over who carries the legacy—the Red Douglases or the Black.

I know that same bent lives in my branch of the Douglas clan. Forget the drama a hundred years ago or even twenty, we play out this pattern today. In the past two years, my dad and I have waged plenty of wars on each other and on ourselves. As his dementia advanced, I picked fights I knew I would lose because I wanted to do things "the right way." One of the early warnings of his mental decline was when I cleaned out his chaotic utility room only to have him yell at me for the better part of an hour and refuse to talk to me for the rest of the day.

But that incident did nothing to deter me from trying to fix things I thought were wrong with my dad. Nor did it deter Dad from being stubborn and cantankerous when I tried to do things for his good. Our fights were never physical, but much emotional blood was shed between us.

But not only were we harmful to each other. We hurt ourselves. Not intentionally, but as grief bubbled up and my anger at the hopelessness of the situation rose, my love came out sideways.

As Dad worsened, I doubled down on caring for both of them. Most of my spare moments went to trying to make their lives a little longer, a little better—even at the expense of my own health.

My doctor's appointments told the tale. After multiple readings of high blood pressure, I was put on medication.

My psychiatrist increased my dose of antidepressants. I put on more weight. Like many caregivers, as Dad's health declined, so did mine.

Sometimes as I would fill Dad's medicine box, I would marvel at how plainly I'd inherited my health problems. High blood pressure meds, antidepressants, and cholesterol medicine were among the prescriptions we shared. Moreover, we shared the same stubborn temper. Even when I gently encouraged Dad to give up driving, he refused, and he insisted no one but Mom and I help care for him. When he eventually lost those fights, that Douglas temper would flare. I can believe he descended from fierce warriors who fought to the bitter end. Dad always went down fighting, against me and even against his own good.

But you can only tear at your own foundation for so long before the house begins to fall.

After a day when Mom's stubbornness joined Dad's over moving to assisted living, I broke. I yelled and I cried and told them if they wouldn't accept the help they needed, I was out. I slammed the door and left in a rage. Halfway home, my anger turned to tears of desperation and prayer. I begged God for help. I felt nudged to turn right toward the local gym. Something had to change. If I couldn't save them, I had to start choosing to save myself.

The shift of repentance can look different in different situations. That day for me, repentance was a shift from choosing death, destruction, and anger to choosing life, healing, and God's mysterious peace. I needed God to make a new heart in me. I needed to learn to love and care for myself, even in my grief.

Evening after evening, Jason and I met at the pool to swim laps. I took my anger and frustration out on the water as my hands slapped through the surface again and again. Eventually, I'd wear myself out and move from curses of frustration to prayers for help and holy comfort. I prayed for God to cleanse me of my anger, to make room in my heart for God's peace. I would end my time in the pool by floating on my back. Giving my body's weight to the water helped me give the weight of my worries to God.

Not only did this new practice of swimming help my blood pressure, but it also helped change my spirit. I was able to keep my temper in difficult interactions with my parents. I saved my hard feelings for the pool, where the water graciously washed them away.

As I walk from the last tower of the Douglas stronghold to the stream running nearby, I meditate on all that the waters of grace have washed away and all that they have brought in. The year of caregiving and the year of grief were hard.

Sometimes I thought the weight of it all would pull me under. But God saw me through. The water kept cleansing away my bitterness and anger, then my grief. Each morning in prayer, I joined the Psalmist in asking God to renew my heart and fill my lips with praise.

Moment by moment, choosing life has brought a bit of resurrection. Of course, for Mom and Dad too. I never doubted that their spirits were leaving me to dwell in God's presence. And for me, too. Joy returns. Life is sweeter. Each day I pick up the bricks of my torn-down self and try to build a life that is pleasing to God. But most of all, I try to rest in the waters of God's abundant grace.

CHAPTER 6

PSALM 23

1 The LORD is my shepherd; I shall not want.
2 He makes me lie down in green pastures;
he leads me beside still waters;
3 He restores my soul.
He leads me in right paths
for his name's sake.

4 Even though I walk through the darkest valley,
I fear no evil,
for you are with me;
your rod and your staff,
they comfort me.

5 You prepare a table before me
in the presence of my enemies;
you anoint my head with oil;
my cup overflows.
6 Surely goodness and mercy shall follow me
all the days of my life,
and I shall dwell in the house of the LORD
my whole life long.

OLD GRAVES

I WALK BY THE crumbling gravestones and read off the dates. They are just visible on the worn, mossy stones. "1734–1796. 1810–45. 1876–1877." We have found our way to St. Bride's Kirk, just outside the Douglas estate. After touring the castle ruins, we stopped at the church and its cemetery to see if we could find the graves of my ancestors.

"I'm not seeing any Douglases, hon. Lots and lots of old graves though." My husband peers over at me from the other end of the churchyard. I start walking towards him. "Yeah, I think some of the oldest Douglas graves are inside the church building, and it's blocked off until they reinforce the old stonework." Jason shrugs. "Well, I guess we can see those graves next visit. Not like they are going anywhere."

I snort a little laugh. One true thing about the dead is that they just keep on being dead. Somewhere under this chuckle is the ache of permanence.

This past year of grief has been hard. First came the actual moments of Mom and Dad's deaths—my brother and I keeping vigil, moistening their lips, holding their hands through the last exhale. Then came the sad phone calls and funerals. Next was the long "year of firsts": first Christmas without them, first birthdays they were not here to celebrate. When Dad's death anniversary rolled around, I breathed a sigh of relief that I had made it through the gauntlet.

But then the hospice brochure arrived—*Grieving Beyond the First Year*—and I realized my journey through grief wasn't over. In some ways, it had only begun. Because the dead keep being dead.

Every milestone we celebrate from here on out will be without them. My parents won't see my kids graduate from college or attend their weddings. One day we will place two roses on a seat instead of seeing their smiling faces in the front row of the bride's side of the church. They will never see me become a grandmother or attend my retirement celebration. Even here in Scotland, I keep wanting to call and tell them what we are seeing and doing. I still get choked up in the grocery store when I pass their favorite foods. Every small and large moment of my life will now be lived without my parents sharing it with me.

"Ready to go, hon? We probably need to find some lunch." Jason stands at the edge of the graveyard as the kids walk to the rental car. I take one last look at all the tombstones—all these people someone loved and lost: parents who died when their children were still young, lovers who died before the shine wore off the wedding rings, children who died before they took their first steps.

I feel my own ache reflected back at me. How long their families must have missed them. How many birthdays and holidays were marked with absence. How many lives had to be lived carrying that ache side by side with joy. Grief leaves a hole because love rooted itself so deeply. How big must the hole be in this world because of all the lives that have been lost?

As we climb the cobbled hill toward the village deli, I try to lift myself out of despair. A conversation with my spiritual director comes to mind. She opened her worn Bible to the 23rd Psalm and said, "I want you to focus on the last part of this psalm." She leaned toward me to make sure I was listening.

"Thou preparest a table before me in the presence of mine enemies: thou anointest my head with oil; my cup runneth over. Surely goodness and mercy shall follow me all the days of my life: and I will dwell in the house of the LORD forever."

She placed her hand over the page for emphasis. "Remember that even when things are difficult and sad, God prepares a table just for you—and you keep on feasting. God pours the healing oil over your head, and your cup runneth over."

This image has come back to me again and again over this past year—how God's kindness finds me even amid my grief, how I am nourished and healed even in the midst of the hard. There is still so much good in this life, so much mercy flowing out of my cup. I feel its warmth wrap around me time and time again. I know that at the heavenly feast, my parents are still with me. I am learning the contours of this new relationship of ours.

As I feast on God's grace here on earth, they feast on God's grace at the banquet. And as *Song of Songs* tells us, love is stronger than death. My parents' love has been sealed upon my heart; death cannot take that away.

As I eat my sandwich, I think of that heavenly feast and the love shared there—of the day I will one day feast with my parents in the great beyond. Until then, I will enjoy the sweetness of this life even as I weep for their absence. I might not be able to call Mom on the phone and tell her they have chicken salad sandwiches in Scotland, but her love is with me as I discover this joy. Her delight is with me even as I ache at her absence.

The dead keep being dead, but somehow, my life goes on.

CHAPTER 7

PSALM 139:1–18

1 O LORD, you have searched me and known me.
2 You know when I sit down and when I rise up;
you discern my thoughts from far away.
3 You search out my path and my lying down
and are acquainted with all my ways.
4 Even before a word is on my tongue,
O LORD, you know it completely.
5 You hem me in, behind and before,
and lay your hand upon me.
6 Such knowledge is too wonderful for me;
it is so high that I cannot attain it.

7 Where can I go from your spirit?
Or where can I flee from your presence?
8 If I ascend to heaven, you are there;
if I make my bed in Sheol, you are there.
9 If I take the wings of the morning
and settle at the farthest limits of the sea,
10 even there your hand shall lead me,
and your right hand shall hold me fast.
11 If I say, “Surely the darkness shall cover me,

and night wraps itself around me,"
12 even the darkness is not dark to you;
the night is as bright as the day,
for darkness is as light to you.

13 For it was you who formed my inward parts;
you knit me together in my mother's womb.
14 I praise you, for I am fearfully and wonderfully made.
Wonderful are your works;
that I know very well.
15 My frame was not hidden from you,
when I was being made in secret,
intricately woven in the depths of the earth.
16 Your eyes beheld my unformed substance.
In your book were written
all the days that were formed for me,
when none of them as yet existed.
17 How weighty to me are your thoughts, O God!
How vast is the sum of them!
18 I try to count them—they are more than the sand;
I come to the end—I am still with you.

KNOWN

WALKING ACROSS THE bridge to Culzean Castle, I keep thinking, *this is so much bigger than I imagined.* We have only driven about fifty miles from the village of Douglas where the ruins of my ancestors' castle lie, but I feel as if I'm in another world. Beyond the castle walls rises a three-story yellow stone mansion set against the edge of the sea. There is nothing ruined about this building. It looks as impressive today as when it was expanded and remodeled in the late 1700s.

As we go inside, a guide greets us with a brochure about the castle. Jason leads us into the dining room. I don't know where to look first—my eyes dart from oil paintings to precious antiques to crystal chandeliers. "Don't forget to look up!" the guide says with a proud smile. A fresco fills the center of the ornately decorated ceiling, and I cannot imagine how many hours were devoted to creating it.

The sitting room is no less ornate. I open the brochure in confusion. "Who in the world could afford all this?" I wonder aloud. I read about David Kennedy, the 10th Earl of Cassilis. "Get this," I say to Jason and the kids. "This place was only the Marquess's summer home. Can you imagine?" My mind tries to reconcile this new information with what I had always assumed about the Scots.

I had always been taught my ancestors were poor and scrappy people—the ones the rich and powerful English picked on. But clearly, some of the lowland Scots were quite rich and powerful themselves. My ancestors moved in circles with the folks who owned this house—and sometimes even fought them for power. Was my family really who I thought they were all this time?

We make assumptions about our families that may or may not be true—and not just the ancestors who lived an ocean away.

I will never forget the day I learned my grandparents had been divorced. I was reading my parents' wedding announcement and couldn't understand why my grandmother was listed with the wrong last name. When I asked Mom to explain, she simply said, "Oh, that was during the time your Grandma divorced your Grandaddy and was married to that other man." I could feel my brain exploding the long-held image I had of two grandparents who had been happily married for sixty years.

The same was true at the end with my parents. I don't know what it is about aging and dying, but sometimes people finally share the stories they carried in silence—the ones that explain what made them who they are. I found myself wondering what life might have been like if I had really known my parents for more of our time together. Even at Mom's funeral, people kept coming up to me to tell me how she had helped them. Never one to make a fuss, Mom kept all those acts of generosity and kindness to herself.

Mom, did I ever really know you?

That question stayed with me long after the funeral.

As I tried to reconcile the mother I thought I knew for fifty years with the clearer picture that emerged after her death, I cried out to God for help. Who can we ever know and be known by if not our own mother who brought us into this world? The re-ordering of her image was disorienting and left me feeling alone and unmoored.

God answered my cry with a line from Psalm 139, "O Lord, you have searched me and known me. You know when I sit down and when I rise up; you discern my thoughts from far away. You search out my path and my lying down and are acquainted with all my ways."

Even if my mom—my sweet, strong, private mom—did not allow her own self to be fully known. And in that, she taught me I should not be fully known, God knew. God knew me as I was being knit in my mother's womb, and God knows me in my grief. God knew me in every stupid fight I had with my mom over things neither of us really understood.

Even as God knows me, God calls me wonderfully made. And even as God knows me, God knows Mom too. And is just as taken with her.

I cannot understand the mysteries of parent-child relationships. How we can love each other so much yet feel so divided sometimes? Why is it impossible to know your own mom? But God understands. And we are held in that common understanding and in that common love and care.

Maybe it is enough that I never knew the fullness of my mom. Some days, I feel I barely know myself.

Sitting on a bench by the duck pond on the Culzean grounds, I look over at my son and daughter. There is much I have shared with them about myself, but much that lies hidden still. And as they become adults, I know there is more they keep hidden from me.

What will we choose to share with each other during the course of this trip? How much truth can our love hold? We walk back to the car to begin the ride back to Glasgow. I ask God to help me let them know how much I love them. If they understand nothing else about their mother, maybe my love will be enough.

For my mom and me at least, it is now so.

CHAPTER 8

PSALM 100

1 Make a joyful noise to the LORD, all the earth.
2 Serve the LORD with gladness;
come into his presence with singing.

3 Know that the LORD is God.
It is he who made us, and we are his;
we are his people and the sheep of his pasture.

4 Enter his gates with thanksgiving
and his courts with praise.
Give thanks to him; bless his name.

5 For the LORD is good;
his steadfast love endures forever
and his faithfulness to all generations.

EVERYDAY

I POKE MY HEAD into a pub near our hotel and am hit by a wall of noise from fans cheering on their team. I look back at Jason, "Um, maybe not tonight? There seems to be a major football game happening, and I don't think I can take that much stimulation right now."

We've only just gotten back to Glasgow after touring my ancestral estate in County Lanarkshire and visiting Culzean Castle. It has been a lot to process in one day. Eli points to a restaurant across the street. "How about spicy chicken?" Jason and Libby cheer. My husband and kids love spicy anything, but spicy chicken is their favorite.

As we walk in the blessedly calm restaurant, I am curious how Glaswegian spicy chicken measures up to the kind we make in the American South. Then I read the story on the menu and realize we are in a restaurant founded by a South African family. After moving to the UK, they missed their beloved peri-peri chicken so much they decided to share it with their new home. Looking around the restaurant, I see all sorts of ethnic backgrounds.

We sit in comfortable silence, waiting for our chicken

plates. A family at the next table catches my eye. Two young boys laugh as they recount their afternoon football game to their dad. My gaze shifts to the table across from them, where a mother chats with her teenage son. Around us sit families of all kinds, out for a quick weeknight dinner.

And a pang of grief hits my chest.

After my parents died, people prepared me to be sad on major holidays. Our hospice chaplain sent me booklets with titles like, "The First Father's Day Without Your Dad." With help from my family and therapist, I got through those days pretty well. I was sad, but okay.

The real gut punches came seemingly out of nowhere. The first time we went out for pizza on a Sunday night. The first Dawgs home game. Those everyday moments hit me harder than the holidays somehow. Maybe because they too were inextricably connected with my parents.

After our children were born, we decided to move to a house twenty minutes from my parents' house and forty-five minutes from Jason's family. Jason's dad was seriously ill with a life-threatening illness, and we wanted our kids to know their grandparents while they still could. The offer of free babysitting didn't hurt either.

Thus, years of weekly dinners began with my folks. When the kids were little, we met at an all-you-can-eat pizza buffet—the kind with games and prizes and unlimited ice cream. The kids had a ball, and my parents relished seeing their grandchildren happy. I was glad for the break from the constant caretaking of my children and the chance for adult conversation.

As the kids grew, our dinners did too. We moved on to local Italian restaurants, plates piled with pasta while the kids filled their grandparents in on their week. After my dad began declining with dementia, we started eating at my folks' house. Mom cooked meals we could all enjoy, and Dad was more comfortable in familiar surroundings. In the last years, when Mom was declining too, we brought takeout pizza to them.

I realize I was incredibly lucky to share so many everyday moments with my parents as an adult. Not everyone gets this opportunity. And honestly, the everyday moments were often my favorite. Without the pressure of a holiday, we were just together sharing life.

After my parents were gone, it would make sense that it was these everyday moments I would miss most.

I wish I could go back and tell myself to enjoy those moments while I had them. To some extent, I did. And to some degree, I knew I was lucky at the time. But there was so much everyday drama that got in the way.

One week, I was mad at Dad again. Another week, Mom would make an unkind comment about my weight. Then I would retaliate the next week with a negative comment about Mom's constant bridge playing. Would she really rather play one more game of bridge a week than spend the afternoon with her grandchildren?

It went on and on. After the fussing years, our visits became overshadowed by my worry about Dad's health and Mom's ability to cope as a caregiver. I couldn't stay present in the joy of a single evening—I was always measuring what might be wrong.

It wasn't always this way. There were some days we were genuinely happy together but looking back, they seem too few. I feel like a character from *Our Town* who wants to go back and shake myself and ask if I knew how lucky I was—to have living parents who loved me and wanted to spend time with me.

But of course, we can never know the value of a Saturday afternoon spent eating pizza and watching football with our family until we see it in hindsight. I guess the only question left is: what can I do with the remaining days of my life?

At my maternal grandmother's funeral, my aunt asked me to read Psalm 100 as part of the service. She told us MaMa read this Psalm every morning of her life. That has always stayed with me. I wonder what I would be like if the first thing I read every morning was a reminder to praise God and celebrate God's goodness and faithfulness in my life and the world.

Maybe I would remember to be grateful for the little things in my life and celebrate the gift of the everyday. What if I went ahead and started doing this right now?

I watch my children eating their spicy chicken and fries. They clearly approve of the peri-peri sauce. I notice the sweat on Jason's brow. I laugh at how he insists on ordering the spiciest choice available at any restaurant.

My heart bursts with love for these imperfect people who make up my family. I am so grateful to be sharing this moment with them. Even though yesterday I got on the kids' nerves, and tomorrow Jason and I will get into an argument, I love them.

What is this miracle we get to be on this earth with other people and share our lives together?

I finish my corn on the cob and wipe my face. I am full in all the best ways. Please, God, if I have learned anything from my grief, let me cherish each day I have with my family on this trip. The kids are growing up and will soon leave the nest fully to live their lives on their own. Let me know how precious each moment of this time is. Even the fussy moments, the tired moments, the messy moments. Let me remember to give thanks for their goodness.

CHAPTER 9

Psalm 30

1 I will extol you, O LORD, for you have drawn me up
and did not let my foes rejoice over me.
2 O LORD my God, I cried to you for help,
and you have healed me.
3 O LORD, you brought up my soul from Sheol,
restored me to life from among
those gone down to the Pit.

4 Sing praises to the LORD, O you his faithful ones,
and give thanks to his holy name.
5 For his anger is but for a moment;
his favor is for a lifetime.
Weeping may linger for the night,
but joy comes with the morning.

6 As for me, I said in my prosperity,
"I shall never be moved."
7 By your favor, O LORD,
you had established me as a strong mountain;
you hid your face;
I was dismayed.

8 To you, O LORD, I cried,
and to the Lord I made supplication:
9 "What profit is there in my death,
if I go down to the Pit?
Will the dust praise you?
Will it tell of your faithfulness?
10 Hear, O LORD, and be gracious to me!
O LORD, be my helper!"

11 You have turned my mourning into dancing;
you have taken off my sackcloth
and clothed me with joy,
12 so that my soul may praise you and not be silent.
O LORD my God, I will give thanks to you forever.

LOCH LOMOND

WE MAKE OUR way through the streets of Balloch in search of an early lunch. Jason motions to a restaurant on our right. "This place looks good, what do y'all think?" The restaurant is open, close to the ferry. Best of all, I can see people eating pastries through the window. We all give a thumbs up and Jason opens the door for me to go through.

"Mom, is it wrong to order a Victoria Sponge for lunch? I've always wanted to try one, and it is on their menu." Libby looks at me with a worried face.

"Sweetie, if pastries for lunch are wrong, I don't want to be right. I'm getting a scone. The description of how they serve it sounds amazing." I close my menu with determination. Before long we are all sipping tea with milk and sugar as we wait for our chosen meals.

"So, is this the Loch Lomond we sang about?" Eli asks. Our kids sang the traditional Scottish folk tune named after this lake at a high school choir competition. Eli starts reciting the lyrics. "*By yon bonnie banks and by yon bonnie braes where the sun shines bright on Loch Lomond, where me and my true love were ever wont to gae, On the bonnie, bonnie banks o' Loch Lomond.*" One of the things I'd most looked forward to on this trip was seeing Loch Lomond with my own eyes. The song makes it sound so beautiful and mysterious, and I love all the Scottish lore.

After eating the last crumbs of our pastry lunch, we walk over near the boat landing. When we get to the bridge over the River Leven, Libby and I stop short. Hundreds of locks line the railings.

"I've heard about this!" Libby exclaims. "Couples come and put locks along bridges to symbolize their everlasting bond." I nod. It seems a fitting gesture at the base of a loch that sings about true love. I can imagine these couples engraving their initials on the lock, closing it over the bridge rails and throwing away the key to say to each other, "No matter what, I will always love you."

There is a lot about Scotland that has affirmed my belief in love—not just romantic love, though Jason has been a dear on this trip, but familial love as well. One saying quoted to me this past year has stayed with me: "Grief is love with nowhere left to go." I don't know how much that saying comforted me on hard days, but I guess it is true. Love is not quenched by death.

I will always love my parents and always miss them while I am on this earth. Our bond is eternal, but that bond doesn't make it easier to be the one left behind.

I think about the legends around the song, "Loch Lomond." How some say it is about two lovers; others say it is a ballad from one prisoner of war to another. The prisoner to be executed sings to the one soon to be freed, "*You take the high road, and I'll take the low road, and I'll be in Scotland afore ye.*" One day, at least in spirit, they will both be in Scotland again.

It comforts me to think about it this way with my

folks. They have taken the fast track to heaven while I still walk the earth. One day we will be reunited in our true home, the LORD's house, where we will dwell for eternity.

But for now, I am walking the highways and byways of life without them, and honestly, some days that just stinks. One of the hardest emotions I've wrestled with in this season of grieving is anger.

I was angry that Mom died and left me to take care of Dad. Sure, Dad was mad too, but he had the luxury of sitting in his recliner and crying for his true love while I got the groceries and paid the bills. I was too busy on the high road to feel properly sad.

As hard as it was to have my dad left alive without Mom—elderly, ill, and heartbroken—I was mad when Dad died three brutal months after her. Again, my brother and I were left to clean up the mess. We went through the house, sorted through their things, and handled matters with their estate.

But it wasn't just their unfinished business I was angry at having to manage without them—it was mine. Now I have to walk through my life facing every up and down with no Mom to call or Dad to cheer me on. No cute red lock with initials on it will make that feel better.

There is no other choice, nothing to do but keep climbing the mountains and navigating the valleys ahead of me. As I told someone when they asked how I was shortly after my parents died, "Well, I can't climb in the grave with them. So I just keep pressing on."

That is what it feels like to be the one left behind on the high road sometimes. You have to keep putting one foot in front of the other whether you like the turn life has taken or not. Because even though your beloved has died, life goes on.

And it sucks.

One thing that kept me going during this time was the promise that there would be better days ahead. Friends who had lost loved ones reached out to me in my time of grief and encouraged me to hang on. "The first year is rough," they would say. "The second year is hard too," they would confess. But then they would assure me that one day things would get easier. Joy would return.

I looked at other friends who lost parents back-to-back and saw that they were now celebrating weddings of grown children and births of new grandchildren. I could imagine the day when my own mourning would be replaced by dancing with joy.

Like the lines of Loch Lomond say, "*But the broken heart it kens nae second spring again, though the waeful may cease frae their grieving.*" I will probably see a "second spring" again. I can imagine the day when new life comes and I am truly happy. It doesn't often feel that way yet, but I am still in the early years of grief. Life will come again. One day grief won't feel so hard.

But even then, I'll miss my loved ones who took the low road. We will always miss them.

As rain begins to drizzle down on us, I take one last look at the locks. They will remain suspended between these banks through rain and shine, spring and fall, bearing witness to the passing of our lives. Like my parents looking down on me from the hereafter, still sending me their love and hopefully still receiving mine. After all, even though they are gone, they still hold the key to my heart.

CHAPTER 10

PSALM 142

1 With my voice I cry to the LORD;
with my voice I make supplication to the LORD.
2 I pour out my complaint before him;
I tell my trouble before him.
3 When my spirit is faint,
you know my way.

In the path where I walk,
they have hidden a trap for me.
4 Look on my right hand and see:
there is no one who takes notice of me;
no refuge remains to me;
no one cares for me.

5 I cry to you, O LORD;
I say, “You are my refuge,
my portion in the land of the living.”
6 Listen to my cry,
for I am brought very low.

Save me from my persecutors,

for they are too strong for me.
7 Bring me out of prison,
so that I may give thanks to your name.
The righteous will surround me,
for you will deal bountifully with me.

NO EASY ROAD

AS WE DRIVE around another curve, my husband hugs the side of the mountain on our left. As we exit the bend, we see yet another car racing towards us, seemingly coming into our already small lane. When Google Maps routed us along Loch Lomond on our way to the Scottish Highlands, we thought it would be a scenic drive. We had no idea how narrow and winding the road would be. Much less that it would be wedged between rock face on one side and a dangerous drop to a valley of water on the other.

My husband grips the steering wheel harder and inhales a sharp breath before asking the question we are all thinking, "How many more miles on this road?" As my son checks Google Maps for mileage, an answer rings out in my head. *Too many. That's how many miles. Too many.* As there are no places to turn around in sight, the only answer is to keep going. I take a deep breath and begin to pray.

Rough roads have been the norm for us these past two years. My husband, Jason, walked by my side as I cared for my mom and dad as they both battled dementia. He stayed close as we walked my mom toward her death from kidney failure, and then cared for my dad until his death soon after. I don't know about him, but I have gotten so tired of hard roads through shadowed valleys.

As we approach another curve, a tour bus appears from around the corner. I cry out as Jason pulls even farther to the left. I put my hand on his shoulder. "I'm so sorry we didn't check directions for an easier road. So sorry you're having to navigate this." Driving a rental car in Scotland for two days has not prepared him for this. He has barely mastered driving on the other side of the road and roundabouts. He was not ready for narrow mountain roads. I question the wisdom of choosing to drive in a foreign land.

Jason offers no response to my statement. He merely keeps his white knuckles on the wheel and drives on. My son consoles, "Five more miles, Dad, you can do this."

When we get to the Isle of Skye, we all take a deep breath. The salty sea air is a balm for the stress of travel. We head off toward shore to let the sight of ocean waves unravel the knots of stress we have accumulated. "No more driving today," my daughter offers. "And tomorrow we just travel down to the fairy pools." We all nod in agreement.

On the way to the fairy pools, we check Google Maps for the best route. Since we are staying at the top of the island there are two ways to go. If we head left, we will go back the way we came, past the Old Man of Storr and Portree. Part of that road is one track and has lots of tourist travel.

If we head right, we drive around the top of the island and down the other side. We all vote for the side with fewer tour buses.

For the first few minutes, the drive is beautiful. We marvel at the beauty of this wild place, the rocky outcrops, the ocean, and the lime-washed farmhouses dotting the bogland.

Then fog rolls up from the ocean on our right, and mist shrouds the island. Jason slows down and keeps his eyes on the small bit of road visible before him. It doesn't help that sheep roam freely on the Isle of Skye. As we come around a bend, a mother sheep and her lamb sit on the side of the road and watch us pass. I wonder if they think we should have turned left when we had the chance. If only the sheep had a staff to guide us.

There were many times while caring for my parents when I wished I had taken another path. If only I could have convinced them to move into assisted living a year ago, someone would have noticed the signs of my mom's kidney disease before it was too late. If I had decided to keep paying round-the-clock sitters to care for my dad at home, he wouldn't have fallen and hit his head while walking to the bathroom in his memory care apartment. If only, if only.

I agonized over every decision I made for them, and yet it seemed like every choice turned out badly. No choice was the right choice. No way was the easy way.

Since we are leaving the Isle of Skye, I ask the hotel clerk the best way to Inverness. "It looks like there are two roads that cut across the Highlands. Which one is the easiest to drive?" She looks at me in surprise. "Well, you are tourists, you have to take the road that goes along Loch Ness, aye?" I try to explain our troubles at Loch Lomond and ask again which road is easier for people not used to driving in Scotland. "It has been a while since I've taken the upper road, but it's fine. A normal road."

We continue to discuss the two roads in the car as we

head off the island. My son pulls them both up on the navigation screen. My daughter dubs them the high road and the low road, and we discuss the merits and drawbacks of each. As we leave the island, Jason says he is feeling better about driving and will take the low road. One mile later he takes a left on the high road.

"J, this is the road through the mountains, the high road. Is this what you wanted to do?" I ask in a tight voice. I'm not sure I can take another day of white-knuckle driving. "Well, maybe I will turn around when I get the chance," he replies. We start climbing up a mountain with rock face on either side of a narrow road. "Looks like we are taking the high road," my son deadpans.

An hour later, I am drowsy and slightly carsick from the switchbacks. The road is not easy, but at least it is quiet. "Hey, a lookout spot," my daughter calls. "Can we stop so I can take some pictures?" Jason and the kids pile out of the car in search of the best views. I lean against the side of the car and take a few deep breaths. It seems there is no easy road in Scotland. Just different versions of hard roads.

As I look out at the valley to the right, I realize just how true that is. Sometimes there is just no good road.

As much as I wanted to choose the right path with my parents, there really wasn't one. Every road we went down was leading through the valley of the shadow of death. No matter what choice I made, they were going to get worse and eventually die. That was always how the story was going to end. And the road to death is rarely if ever easy.

If they had moved to assisted living two years ago, it would have been hard. They would have missed home and Dad's dementia would have immediately gotten worse. I knew that their staying home was hard. I watched them struggle with daily tasks for a year before Mom suddenly and seemingly inexplicably got worse.

Moving Dad to memory care was hard. He was miserable in new surroundings, and I constantly felt guilty for making the choice. But having him at home with live-in caregivers was going to be hard too. There was so much to manage, and honestly, he would have eventually fallen and hurt himself even at home.

Sometimes the road will always be hard no matter what path we choose. It will feel like there are snares on our left and on our right. All we can do is keep walking through the difficult valley and take comfort where we can. For we never walk through it alone. I was fortunate to have Jason by my side as I walked through the dark valley with my parents. He not only cared for me during that time, but he cared for them as well. But more than that, God was with me—watching over me as I navigated the hard paths and walking beside me when the way grew tough. That didn't make the road any easier, but I knew I would make it through to the other side.

CHAPTER 11

PSALM 121

1 I lift up my eyes to the hills—
from where will my help come?
2 My help comes from the LORD,
who made heaven and earth.

3 He will not let your foot be moved;
he who keeps you will not slumber.
4 He who keeps Israel
will neither slumber nor sleep.

5 The LORD is your keeper;
the Lord is your shade at your right hand.
6 The sun shall not strike you by day
nor the moon by night.

7 The Lord will keep you from all evil;
he will keep your life.
8 The LORD will keep
your going out and your coming in
from this time on and forevermore.

SURPRISES

AS WE LEAVE Loch Lomond and the Trossachs National Park, we turn left onto Highway A82. The land around us opens up and we climb in altitude. Before we know it, we are in the mountains. I had heard that Scotland was a country of mountains. I had even read about the Munros, the 282 peaks over 3,000 feet. None of what I learned prepared me for what we see.

After each bend of the road, another gorgeous vista opens before us. Range after range of green-grey mountains rises before our eyes, each one unique. Though these mountains and the Appalachians that formed the backdrop of my life were shaped in the same geological moment of creation, they are worlds apart. While the Appalachians are wrapped in trees, these mountains are open, mossy moorlands. With nothing to block the horizon, every curve and rocky ridge shows itself against the clear blue sky.

When we find an overlook, we pull over and park. The temperature has dropped around ten degrees, so we put on our windbreakers and step out onto the moors. My son heads off towards the nearest rise while my daughter takes the lens cap off her camera. Jason stands nearby while I take a seat on a boulder. It is all I can do to drink in the sights around me. As the peat-scented wind whips my hair, a cloud drifts over the ridge, playing out a drama of shadow and light before my eyes. The beauty mesmerizes me.

For the next hour, we drive and stop, drive and stop. At some pullovers, hikers head out for a day of exploration. At others, travelers like us are blown away by God's amazing showcase of glory. I feel small against the grandeur of this landscape. I lift my eyes to take in the ridges around us.

At some point, I try to put words to our experience. "It's like a giant present we keep unwrapping as we go. I never imagined it would be this beautiful." My family nods in agreement. This stretch of mountains heading into Glencoe is a wonderful surprise.

The great thing about surprises is their unexpectedness. When you receive an anticipated present, you appreciate it, but you treasure a wonderful surprise.

I think about the happy surprises during the last two years of sickness and grief. There were good days or tender times when light broke through the darkness. I had a friend tell me about this phenomenon. "It will be hard," she said, "but look for the gifts. They'll come when you least expect them."

And the gifts did come. Some days Dad was lucid, grabbing my hand and telling me how much he loved and appreciated me, and how proud he was of the person I'd become. Some days Mom was tender and affectionate, showing just how much love and joy I brought into her life. Even the nights we laughed and cheered over college football or game shows shone like bright lights in an otherwise dark time.

These pleasant surprises, these bright lights, carried

me through the hard times. The promise of another one around the corner kept me going when I wasn't sure how much I had left to give.

And the harder things became, the more precious each gift felt. The two weeks Mom was on hospice were heartbreaking, but they were also full of friends and family telling Mom how much she meant to them and by extension, how much we meant to them. They came with food and flowers and cards. They told stories about Mom I had never heard, like how she had sent a card and gift for every childhood birthday of her nieces and nephews. These stories reminded me of truths about her I had forgotten. By midweek, I learned not to refuse company. Calls and visits kept rolling in, each carrying another small surprise of comfort and memory.

Things somehow become clearer at the end. All the petty mother/daughter fights we'd had faded. I finally saw her for who she really was—who she had always been. A woman who had fought for everything she ever had and who wanted to make things a little easier for her daughter, even when her idea of easy wasn't the same as mine. And the love between us wrapped around her sick room, holding us tightly. Love that was so much bigger than any squabble or disagreement kept us close together in the shade of God's hand.

The only thing I wished at the end was that I had realized how precious my mother's life was years earlier. Why did it take her fading away for me to see how beautiful she was? I kept lifting my eyes to her face to memorize its contours.

I guess that's how it goes sometimes. It takes the shadows to show us how wonderful the light is. We only recognize this when the surprise gift of understanding appears, and we are grateful it came at all.

As we leave Glencoe, I think about Mom and Dad. I hope somewhere they know I'm seeing this beauty. I hope they know how grateful I am for this life they gave me, a life where I get to experience such awe and wonder. And how grateful I remain to be their child. How blessed I am to be kept in their love even after their death.

When we get to the bed and breakfast in Fort William, we walk across the street to the beach. Someone has built a rock cairn there. As the kids explore, I consider adding a rock to the top of the pile, but I am too tired, too emotionally spent to try. Still, I can't help thinking about Ebenezers, those 'stones of help' in the Bible. The way we mark moments when God brings us through hard times. I mentally raise my Ebenezer to God for carrying me through the haze of grief into new life. I raise a marker to my parents for all they gave me and how much they shaped the person I am today. I think about how they've arrived in their heavenly home and no longer have to hurt and suffer. And I am so glad, so grateful for it all.

I sit a while longer, gazing up at the hills beyond the loch. The lines of Psalm 121 come back to me, "I lift up my eyes to the hills—from where will my help come? My help comes from the LORD who made heaven and earth." At times, I doubted there could be enough help to get me through the onslaught of the past two years. But God was faithful, and the streams of mercy kept flowing over me. Day by hard day, we walked through the valley. And we didn't just make it through—we had some wonderful, surprising, grace-filled days along the way.

As I get up from the beach to return to the bed and

breakfast for dinner, my heart fills. I have no idea how to express my thanks to God for all the gifts I have been given or for how God has watched over me in the good and bad alike. Then I remember what God wants most of all. Not a rock placed upon a pile, but the gift of my heart, my love, and my life. I bring to mind my favorite hymn, "Come Thou Fount of Every Blessing," lift my soul and pray, "Here is my heart, oh take and seal it. Seal it for thy courts above."

CHAPTER 12

PSALM 51:10–17

10 Create in me a pure heart, O God,
and renew a steadfast spirit within me.
11 Do not cast me from your presence
or take your Holy Spirit from me.
12 Restore to me the joy of your salvation
and grant me a willing spirit, to sustain me.

13 Then I will teach transgressors your ways,
so that sinners will turn back to you.
14 Deliver me from the guilt of bloodshed, O God,
you who are God my Savior,
and my tongue will sing of your righteousness.

15 Open my lips, LORD,
and my mouth will declare your praise.
16 You do not delight in sacrifice, or I would bring it;
you do not take pleasure in burnt offerings.
17 My sacrifice, O God, is a broken spirit;
a broken and contrite heart
you, God, will not despise.

WIND

THE TEMPERATURE HAS dropped ten degrees since the last time we stopped to view the mountains along Highway A82. We've given up on making good time and stop frequently to take in the wonder of these mountains that seem to stretch on forever. As we walk out of the car park onto the grass, a gust of wind slams into us. Any lethargy left in me is blown away and I am fully awake.

"Time to put on our jackets!" I grab the windbreaker that lives in my backpack for the duration of this trip. I had read we would experience four seasons in a day while in Scotland. I had read about the ever-present threat of rain. I don't remember reading about the wind.

I look over at Jason, wincing as the cold air pummels his face. "Downright blustery, isn't it?" he asks. I nod and glance at our children. They run towards the mountains, laughing as if they don't even notice the wind. Their hair dances behind them, a perfect picture of joy.

I remember what it felt like to be that age—when the wind felt bracing or invigorating, never blustery. A good blast of cold air made me feel alive. Nowadays, a wind this strong and this cold makes me want to admire the mountains from inside the car. But I refuse to give in to my desire to stay sheltered from the barrage of wind.

In part, my stubbornness comes from not wanting to feel old. Ever since turning fifty, I've tried to prove my youth by continuing to do things I used to do. I trained for this trip for six months, walking three miles multiple times weekly and hiking on weekends, trying to renew my muscle strength and vitality. I want to keep up with the kids as we explore Scotland's cities and hike its wilderness.

But it isn't just my muscles I'm trying to keep supple. I'm trying to stretch my soul too. It would be so easy to say I've seen enough change and settle into my ways. I often catch myself leaning that direction when someone younger does something I never would have considered. But how does that stiffness help anyone?

So when the wind blows, I try not to stiffen my neck against it. For the wind is never really just wind anyway; it is change.

Just look at the hills around us. Wind has carved them over thousands of thousands of years. Blast after blast softened their rough edges until these mountains became a hiker's dream. I wonder what plans the wind has for me. And how many years it will take to wear down my rough edges?

I think about the multiple meanings of wind in biblical languages. Both *ruah* and *pneuma* shift between wind, breath, and Spirit—sometimes meaning all three at once. That's why I love Pentecost so much. The Spirit comes like a rushing wind, stirring the disciples and calling them into something new.

I miss being excited about God's Spirit calling me to new things. I've felt the winds stirring in my life this last year and prayed for God to guide me, but I'm also afraid of what lies ahead. I am so tired; I don't know if I have the energy for anything new.

To be fair, the winds of change have been strong lately. They've moved past blustery and into full-on gales. I wouldn't wish losing two parents and their childhood home within six months on anyone. It's too much at once. When I look back over the past year, it feels like I was hit by a hurricane. After all of that change, aren't I allowed a season of soft winds?

But of course that much change keeps shifting things inside me. You can't lose that much of your foundation without aftershocks. I never understood this part of grief before. I'd watched others lose a close family member or friend and suffer aftershocks. A year later they would go through a divorce or change careers. I struggled to see how one loss could set the others in motion.

And then my own house was blown down by the wind. Loss rearranges things in your own soul. You're not the same person anymore, and your life afterward won't be the same either. When that truth settled in, I was terrified. I didn't want my life to fall down into ruins like the Douglas castle.

My biggest fear, of course, was losing Jason. I don't know how I could survive losing my one remaining anchor. I clung to him even as I picked fights out of grief. So far he's held me through every push and pull. Then came intrusive thoughts about the kids. I tracked them on Google Maps when they traveled. God wouldn't take my parents and then my kids… right? If my anchors were taken from me in the midst of these storms, I was afraid I would be lost forever.

But storms teach strange lessons. In the worst weather, sailors sometimes have to pull up the anchor—not because it failed, but because the only way to survive is to move with the waves. The anchor is still there, still steady, still doing its job. It just looks different in a storm. Maybe grief is like that too. Maybe part of getting through it is trusting that even when I can't hold on to my anchors the way I want to, I'm still held.

I know the changes ahead are probably both bigger and smaller than losing another family member. They're happening at my core. It's not just my life that's changing—I'm changing.

I pray to God the changes will be good ones.

Each morning as I pray Morning Prayer, I beg these words to be true: "Create in me a clean heart, O God. And put a new and right spirit within me." May that right Spirit, that right *ruah* blow on my tired heart and make it new. Make it better. Make it whole.

Maybe that's part of what's changing—that my broken self will be made whole again, but whole in a new way. I don't know yet. I'm still new at this grief. I can only trust and hope that God is in it, and in me. That God will smooth out the hurts of the past years and fashion me into something useful for the future.

As the kids walk back towards us, I take out my phone for a family photo. I want to remember this moment—these wild, worn mountains and this ever-blowing wind. As my hair whips across my face, I smile into the camera. I don't know what changes are coming, but I will trust the process. Let the wind come. Let it soften me, mold me, make me new. I don't know who I will become, but I trust the Spirit of God to fall as fresh on me not only today, but always.

CHAPTER 13

PSALM 3

1 O LORD, how many are my foes!
Many are rising against me;
2 many are saying to me,
"There is no help for you in God."

3 But you, O LORD, are a shield around me,
my glory, and the one who lifts up my head.
4 I cry aloud to the Lord,
and he answers me from his holy hill.

5 I lie down and sleep;
I wake again, for the LORD sustains me.
6 I am not afraid of ten thousands of people
who have set themselves against me all around.

7 Rise up, O LORD!
Deliver me, O my God!
For you strike all my enemies on the cheek;
you break the teeth of the wicked.

8 Deliverance belongs to the LORD;
may your blessing be on your people!

UNPREPARED

I STUDY MY SON'S expression as we wait to cross the highway between Loch Lochy and our bed and breakfast. We'd spent the afternoon walking along the crystalline shore, admiring the moss-green mountains surrounding Fort William. But now, instead of a shining look of awe, worry creases his young face.

"You okay, bud?" I ask.

He exhales. "I'm stressed about tonight's dinner."

The reason our travel agent booked this particular B&B isn't the accommodations—it's the food. The chef, the owner's son, runs a Michelin-recommended restaurant. Tonight, along with twelve other guests we'll be treated to a fine-dining experience in the hotel's intimate dining room.

"I don't feel ready for this—like I am out of my league. I haven't been to many nice restaurants. And all those other people will be around us, looking at me."

I nod; he's not wrong. We're usually a pizza-and-burgers family when we eat out, so he has not had many chances to practice fine-dining etiquette. And after the owner scolded him about wearing his backpack while being surrounded by expensive decorations, I understand.

I try to reassure him. "You packed a nice outfit, so you'll look the part. And honestly, if you act with kindness and respect, people will forgive you for using the wrong fork. Sometimes we learn by doing—even if we mess up."

He looks unconvinced, but there is not much else to do. We cross back over to the B&B to get ready for tonight's meal. I feel for him because I know what it feels like to be thrown into the deep end before you really know how to swim.

When I first started helping Mom take care of Dad, it was hard but I felt prepared. I was a forty-year-old woman raising two children. I could support and help care for Dad. That was in my wheelhouse. But when Mom went downhill and I was taking care of two parents, one of whom was starting to be seriously ill, I began to feel surrounded by the responsibilities that piled up around me.

I was not a nurse. I had never cared for a critically ill or dying person. And all of a sudden forty-nine felt really young. I kept looking around for someone older and wiser than myself. But it turns out there was no one else who was going to do this job. As young and unprepared as I felt, this was up to me. Prepared or not, I could feel God calling me to care for my parents at their end.

The hospice team was incredibly supportive. The nurses taught me how to administer morphine and Haldol to Mom. They trained me on how to use and maintain an oxygen machine. Our CNAs taught me how to give Mom a sponge bath and safely roll her when changing her bedding. I joked that pretty soon I could enroll in nursing school. I was getting enough on-the-job training for sure. Still sometimes in the night, I would panic about what I knew lay ahead.

Even with all the training, I never felt confident in

what I was doing. Who was I to be making life-or-death decisions for my mom? Thankfully, she had been very clear in her advance directive about her end-of-life wishes. But still, the enormity of it all overwhelmed me.

But sickness and death do not care about our feelings. They are not concerned whether people in the room feel prepared for the course they take.

As things got more serious, I tried to summon all the strength I had. "I am a Southern woman," I told myself. "A steel magnolia. We are the people who handle the hard stuff. We get things done." I tried to cut off my emotions and focus on what Mom needed. And then there was Dad. He was as lost and scared as he could be. I kept watch over him as much as possible and encouraged our CNAs and other family members to keep him company.

But at night when I went home, the emotions hit me. How was this happening to us? How would I ever have the strength and ability to walk with Mom to the shores of death and then pick up Dad after she was gone? It all felt like too much. I felt too young, too incapable for all of this responsibility.

But what else was there to do?

So I prayed. I prayed for strength. I prayed for wisdom. I prayed for the courage to do the hard things even when I was scared I was doing them wrong. I prayed for grace when I did them wrong. As the end neared, my focus sharpened on Mom. While I cared for her, I could feel God's Spirit moving through me. Even as I faced the fiercest foe of my life, God lifted my head to meet the enemy eye to eye. I would not back down.

In the end, death took Mom. Of course it did—that was always how this story would end. But I found the courage to do what needed doing until Mom breathed her last. For me, the goal was simple: to hold her hand and give back the love she had poured into me for so long.

Even now, I don't know if I made every right choice or provided care in all the right ways for my mother at the end. But I am proud that I did my best. In a time when I felt scared and inadequate, I rose up to be the best daughter I knew how to be. Sometimes that's all we can do—give our best and ask for grace. For the God who shields is also the God who forgives.

At dinner, I sit beside my son. We both order the butternut squash ravioli as our main entree. I can feel his tension, but he isn't letting his anxiety prevent him from enjoying what is the best pasta either of us has ever tasted. He lifts his head to look at the beautiful surroundings in between bits of pasta. I'm too busy enjoying my own dinner to notice if he is using the right silverware or not. I take a sip of wine and watch the sun set over the loch. This is a small, beautiful moment, and I am proud of him for finding the courage to enter into it.

Sometimes life comes at us too fast and too hard. We find ourselves facing things we feel unprepared for. I hope he remembers not to back down from hard things out of fear. Sometimes all we can do is pray for help, lift our heads, and do our best.

CHAPTER 14

PSALM 90

1 LORD, you have been our dwelling place
in all generations.
2 Before the mountains were brought forth
or ever you had formed the earth and the world,
from everlasting to everlasting you are God.

3 You turn us back to dust
and say, "Turn back, you mortals."
4 For a thousand years in your sight
are like yesterday when it is past
or like a watch in the night.

5 You sweep them away; they are like a dream,
like grass that is renewed in the morning;
6 in the morning it flourishes and is renewed;
in the evening it fades and withers.

7 For we are consumed by your anger;
by your wrath we are overwhelmed.
8 You have set our iniquities before you,
our secret sins in the light of your countenance.

9 For all our days pass away under your wrath;
our years come to an end like a sigh.
10 The days of our life are seventy years
or perhaps eighty, if we are strong;
even then their span is only toil and trouble;
they are soon gone, and we fly away.

11 Who considers the power of your anger?
Your wrath is as great as the fear that is due you.
12 So teach us to count our days
that we may gain a wise heart.

13 Turn, O LORD! How long?
Have compassion on your servants!
14 Satisfy us in the morning with your steadfast love,
so that we may rejoice and be glad all our days.
15 Make us glad as many days as you have afflicted us
and as many years as we have seen evil.
16 Let your work be manifest to your servants
and your glorious power to their children.
17 Let the favor of the LORD our God be upon us
and prosper for us the work of our hands—
O prosper the work of our hands!

DEATH AND DEFEAT

AS WE EXIT the parking lot at the Glenfinnan viaduct, I see the Jacobite monument off to our left. I don't ask Jason to pull in to visit. Instead, as we drive by, I notice how the Jacobite soldier stands alone against the backdrop of Loch Shiel and the highland mountains. I war with myself over not stopping. The kids really should know this part of Scotland's history. The Jacobite rising against English invaders is a crucial turning point in the country's history.

I rationalize that we wouldn't have time to enjoy the monument. We have to be at the ferry by eleven, so any further stops on the way would make us rush to board. The real truth lies deeper. For me, the defeat is just too sad.

The Scottish had seen their loss of independence to England coming. King James had been overthrown in 1688 and by 1707 Scotland and England were officially united. All during this time there were protests and skirmishes with James trying to take back rule with the help of his supporters, the Jacobites. By the time Bonnie Prince Charlie sailed back to Scotland, in '45, much blood had already been shed.

But it is hard to give up on a dream. And it is nearly

impossible to give up a way of life you have loved deeply. So once again when the call of the pipes went out, the Jacobites rallied.

I get their passion. For two years I fought tooth and nail to keep my way of life. The life of a daughter to living, loving parents. These battles may not have involved guns or swords, but I warded off the specter of death any way I could. I accompanied my parents to doctor's appointments, managed their medication, bought them healthy groceries, and hired helpers to sit with them during the day. I tried anything I could to improve their chance of living more and better days.

I fought until I was bloodied by the battle.

I neglected my own health and quality of life. Some days I hardly cared. I kept hearing the call of the pipes to care for my parents as best I possibly could. To preserve our life together.

I would tell myself that I knew the end was coming. I would tell others I was pre-grieving their death. But my actions showed I was having an awfully hard time letting go. And who can blame me? Who wants to let go of parents they love and have been loved by?

So, like the Jacobites, I fought until the end.

As we continue driving through the Highlands, I wonder what the Jacobite soldiers must have felt as they lined up for their last battle at Culloden. They had been fighting hard for a year and were surely tired. As they set up for this particular fight with the English, it seemed they might be outmanned and outgunned. Were they scared? Angry? Sad? Did they ever think of turning tail and running?

When I came to the end with Mom, death came faster and stronger than I expected. After watching her decline rapidly over a month with no answers from her doctor, I took her to the emergency room. After some initial diagnostics, we were told she was in kidney failure. She might have two weeks left. Still in shock from this blow, I asked for a hospice referral. If Mom only had as many days left as fingers on my hand, we were going to make those days count.

Once home, we turned her bedroom into a comfortable and efficient place to nurse her. I went to the grocery store and bought a mix of Jello, Gatorade, and food for the company we had already invited to come hold vigil with Mom. Since the early daffodils were flowering, I found vases and decorated my parents' bedroom with cheerful yellow blooms. Death may come, but it would have to fight its way through the fence of love we built around Mom.

The next few days were spent trying to get the most out of each moment. We visited with family and called friends on the phone. My aunt helped me give Mom a sponge bath. The nurse's aide helped me fix her hair. Thankfully, the manicure Mom got with my daughter over Christmas break was holding up. If my always proper mother was going to face death, she was going to look like a proper Southern belle while doing it.

Late at night, I would turn to prayer. Where was God in this last battle with death? I had studied enough Scripture to know that God does not promise us victory in every battle and certainly has not promised us victory over physical death. Though Christ promises us eternal life, the shell of our bodies is born to perish. As the Psalmist tells us, we are mortals who, like grass, wither and fade away.

Mom had lived eighty-five good years. Fifty of those with a loving daughter by her side. What more did I want for her? What more did I want for me?

I guess all I knew at the time was I didn't want my mother to die. And who would? Our moms are the first thing we know. What can there be of life after they are gone?

As Mom moved closer to the precipice of death, she was not afraid. She uttered her deceased sister's name and lifted her arms to the heavens while slipping in and out of consciousness. She seemed for all the world ready to move on to the afterlife. She was ready to soar with the eagles. But I was scared. Who would I even be when I left this vigil a motherless child?

Mercifully, God drew near as we kept vigil. I could feel the Holy Spirit surrounding Mom. And surrounding me. I prayed Compline aloud by Mom's bedside. Finally, in the wee hours of the night, Mom exhaled her last breath.

It took several days for the reality of death to set in for me. When the numbness left, all I could feel was deeply tired and sad. Getting out of bed and putting one foot in front of the other was a monumental effort. But I kept going. What else could I do?

A week after Mom's death, I went back to work with my campus ministry group. My smile didn't reach my eyes yet, but eating and talking with the students was good for my soul. When we prayed Compline as a group, the closing prayer stuck with me. "Be present, O merciful God, and protect us through the hours of this night, so that we who are wearied by the changes and chances of this life may rest in your eternal changelessness."

I had been through one of the biggest changes of my life. I had lost my mom. But even so, the changeless presence of God was with me, helping me walk out of the valley of the shadow of death onto a new path. I remembered the promise that God is my dwelling place from everlasting to everlasting. The eternal God would have to hold my hand and give me strength to navigate my way in this unfamiliar territory.

As we neared the ferry landing, I thought about all the changes the Highland Scots had been forced to face. After the loss at Culloden, the English cracked down. The clan system was abolished. Tartans were outlawed. Gaelic was banned. A whole way of life was forbidden in an attempt to crush the spirit of Scotland. And yet, somehow, the highlanders persevered. Many left for America in search of opportunity. But even more stayed, figuring out how to live on in a homeland that no longer looked the same.

Over the past few days, we've learned that even now Scotland still talks about independence. Another referendum is always somewhere on the horizon. Polls show the country divided. And yet, over time, Scotland found a way forward—not by forgetting its past, but by carrying it into the future. Again, given the circumstance what else could it do?

I think about how I have only recently begun to feel more confident in my life without Mom. I wake up each day more ready to face my new world. I try to keep some of the old ways with me—using the last of Mom's lipstick and still cooking some of her favorite dishes. Holidays are different now. Even my weekly trips to the grocery store feel strange when I shop solo. Still I press on. With the help of the God who sees me through good days and bad, I walk into this new life.

CHAPTER 15

PSALM 116:1–7, 12–19

1 I love the LORD because he has heard
my voice and my supplications.
2 Because he inclined his ear to me,
therefore I will call on him as long as I live.
3 The snares of death encompassed me;
the pangs of Sheol laid hold on me;
I suffered distress and anguish.
4 Then I called on the name of the Lord,
"O Lord, I pray, save my life!"

5 Gracious is the LORD and righteous;
our God is merciful.
6 The LORD protects the simple;
when I was brought low, he saved me.
7 Return, O my soul, to your rest,
for the Lord has dealt bountifully with you.

12 What shall I return to the LORD
for all his bounty to me?
13 I will lift up the cup of salvation
and call on the name of the LORD;

14 I will pay my vows to the LORD
in the presence of all his people.
15 Precious in the sight of the LORD
is the death of his faithful ones.
16 O Lord, I am your servant;
I am your servant, the child of your serving girl.
You have loosed my bonds.
17 I will offer to you a thanksgiving sacrifice
and call on the name of the LORD.
18 I will pay my vows to the LORD
in the presence of all his people,
19 in the courts of the house of the LORD,
in your midst, O Jerusalem.
Praise the LORD!

FERRIES

A SEAGULL FLIES OVERHEAD as we cut through the waters of the Sound of Sleat. Our travel agent booked us on the Caledonian MacBrayne ferry to travel from the mainland to the islands. As a lifelong lover of boats and waterways, I've come to the ferry's top deck for our crossing.

The sea-salt air whips through my hair as I gaze over the horizon. To my left, the water stretches out past the islands farther than I can see. Ahead, I spot a fuzzy blue mound between the water and the clouds: the Isle of Skye.

There is something magical about a ferry ride to me. For the next half hour, we will be in a liminal time—that in-between space where we've left the mainland but aren't yet docked on the island. We sail in a soft space where strange things can happen.

This is why writers and myth-makers throughout history have used ferry crossings as a metaphor. Tolkien has the hobbits cross a ferry when they finally leave the Shire on their way to Bree. The ancient Greeks believed the dead crossed the river Styx on a ferry on their way to the underworld.

It makes sense. There is no more liminal space than that between life and death.

I did not always think of death as a transition. Probably because I had never sat vigil when someone died. My Grandaddy died while I was away at school, my Grandma in the ICU, and my MaMa in a nursing home in another city. I never had the chance to hold their hand in their last hours.

Maybe that's why we chose hospice when Mom was diagnosed with terminal kidney failure. I know in many ways I was lucky with my mom's death. She lived a long life into her mid-eighties, stayed active until the very end, and died a natural death in her own bedroom. Though I knew caring for her at home meant keeping a vigil in her final days, nothing could have prepared me for what that experience would actually be like.

A lot of it was hard. Watching Mom stop eating and drinking and slowly waste away in a hospital bed was excruciating. Each day her ability to speak and converse diminished, and it felt even harder. Seeing death close in around Mom broke my heart.

But there was good in that transition too. She looked peaceful and at ease lying in her room with family around her. She even seemed happy as she faded from us—though I'm not sure we were always the reason for that.

There were times when Mom seemed checked out from us and present somewhere else. She spoke the names of deceased loved ones and lifted her arms towards the sky. I know many people would say these actions were caused by the morphine we were giving her or by her body's physical response to the lack of oxygen as it shut down. But I choose to believe Mom was beginning her transition to the hereafter.

The afternoon before my mom died, her hospice nurse confirmed Mom's breathing pattern had changed, and that she would likely be gone by the next morning. My brother and I nodded and made plans to spend the rest of the night with Mom. After a couple of hours of us listening to her breathe, Mom's caregiver encouraged us to take a break for dinner and rotate shifts. It would be a long night.

After Dad went to bed and my brother lay down for a rest, I pulled up the Book of Common Prayer on my phone, opened the service of Compline, and began to pray aloud by Mom's bedside, "The Lord Almighty grant us a peaceful night and a perfect end. Our help is in the name of the Lord; the maker of heaven and earth." As I read the Psalms and prayed the final prayer service of the day, my fear began to melt. God was with us. God was with Mom. God had Mom. I could feel it in my bones.

As the hours stretched on, a deep peace fell over the house. Mom continued to breathe softer and softer in the stillness of the wee hours. It felt like she was being slowly, slowly ushered from our realm into another place. A holy place.

Around three in the morning, my brother woke me to tell me Mom's breathing had changed again. Her breath was rattling harder now, but she showed no distress. We called the hospice nurse to find out what to do. She told us she was on her way, as the end was near. There was nothing we could do now other than hold her hand and pray.

Less than an hour later, Mom breathed her last. It was so gentle and so quiet I could not even name the moment of her last exhale. She was gone, but I could not cry. I felt only amazement at the peace that settled over me at her passing. I knew within myself that Mom had been freed from the earthly chains of her sick body. She had risen up on the wings of dawn and gone to be fully with God.

And God had come so near to us in the process. What I thought would be the saddest moment in my life turned out to be the most precious.

I held onto this feeling as we prepared for her funeral. Her pastor would read Revelation chapter twenty-one at her funeral and a friend would sing "I'll Fly Away." Mom's good life was a gift to give thanks for, as was her good death. She had been safely ferried from earth to heaven, and though I would miss her, I was so glad she was healed and safe with God.

Back on the ferry, I see someone point to the water below. A dolphin has come to swim beside us. Joyful passengers crowd around and take videos of this everyday miracle. I feel a little wink from God as we make this crossing. The God who made the mountains and the seas cares about us. God's compassionate mercy and unfailing goodness wash over me again. "Precious in the sight of the LORD is the death of his faithful servants." And precious in the sight of the LORD are our lives as well. In gratitude, I lift up these words from the Psalms, "Truly I am your servant, LORD; I serve you just as my mother did; you have freed me from my chains. Praise the LORD."

CHAPTER 16

PSALM 42

1 As a deer longs for flowing streams,
so my soul longs for you, O God.
2 My soul thirsts for God,
for the living God.
When shall I come and behold
the face of God?
3 My tears have been my food
day and night,
while people say to me continually,
"Where is your God?"

4 These things I remember,
as I pour out my soul:
how I went with the throng
and led them in procession to the house of God,
with glad shouts and songs of thanksgiving,
a multitude keeping festival.
5 Why are you cast down, O my soul,
and why are you disquieted within me?
Hope in God, for I shall again praise him,
my help and my God.

6 My soul is cast down within me;
therefore I remember you
from the land of Jordan and of Hermon,
from Mount Mizar.
7 Deep calls to deep
at the thunder of your torrents;
all your waves and your billows
have gone over me.
8 By day the LORD commands his steadfast love,
and at night his song is with me,
a prayer to the God of my life.

9 I say to God, my rock,
"Why have you forgotten me?
Why must I walk about mournfully
because the enemy oppresses me?"
10 As with a deadly wound in my body,
my adversaries taunt me,
while they say to me continually,
"Where is your God?"

11 Why are you cast down, O my soul,
and why are you disquieted within me?
Hope in God, for I shall again praise him,
my help and my God.

THIRSTY

MY BROW FURROWS as I look out at the Portree harbor. I let out a sharp sigh. I am not even sure why I'm so angry right now; I only know that I am. My head feels as full of threatening grey clouds as the sky. And since the Isle of Skye is well named, that's a lot of angry clouds.

The tension started on the ferry ride over from Mallaig. I wanted to stand on the ship's bow and watch the waves. But my family stayed inside the cabin and made jokes about all the car alarms going off on the ferry. Our moods collided.

Tempers rose as we had to navigate exiting the ferry and driving Skye's small but crowded roads. My anger erupted when we started discussing lunch plans and how far it was to the hotel. Should we visit Portree on the way to the hotel or come back for dinner? It was a small question really, but it sparked big feelings.

As I sit on a well-placed bench and meditate on the weather of the island and my heart, I realize I am mostly tired. We have been road-tripping through Scotland for days. We have had early mornings in hotel breakfast rooms, long drives on strange roads, and visited countless sites. The wear and tear of traveling in a foreign country, in a different time zone with three other people, is getting to me. I take a deeper breath and pray for rest.

Arriving at the hotel, my children and I decide to take a walk while my husband goes for a run. I tell my son and daughter to go ahead of me on the path and that I'll meet them at the shore's edge. As I sink into a slow pace, I look over at the mountains. The weather has passed, as it so often does in Scotland, and the green hills pop against the azure sky. I pray for my internal weather to clear just as quickly. They say in Scotland, if you don't like the weather, wait fifteen minutes and it will change. I fear I've become just as moody on this trip through the land of my ancestors. There is so much to feel that I can't process it all without my emotions bubbling out.

My poor family should be used to my moods by now. I feel like I've been carrying this crankiness for years. Between the physical exhaustion of caring for my aging parents and the emotional exhaustion of navigating all the choices that come up as we walk through the valley of the shadow of death, I've been a worn-out mess. I've tried to take care of myself. My husband and I started swimming laps at a local pool a few nights a week. The combination of cool water and cardiovascular exercise helped. I walk my two dogs regularly, much to their enjoyment. The fresh air and their wagging tails usually perk up my mood.

But sometimes, sometimes it isn't enough. Some days all the exercise and fresh air in the world cannot soothe my weary soul.

There are times when I need to get away for a day or two and spend time communing with God. When my anger and resentment get too great to handle, I know I need a day reading the Psalms at my favorite retreat center or a quick trip to the mountains. Even an afternoon praying in my church's gardens helps. Like the Psalmist, my dry, thirsty soul needs to soak in the living waters of the God who brings new life.

As I meander closer to the ocean before me, I think about the vastness of God's waters. Bigger even than the Atlantic, God's grace is always there to hold me and wash my wounded heart. I pray for the waters of grace to rise and revive me again, here in this land of water and wonder.

Breathing the salty air deep into my lungs, I pour out my soul to God. I breathe deep, remembering the breath, the spirit, that gives life. I lament again how hard the past few years have been and how much it took out of me. I pray for God to heal my grief and plant a seed of new life in me.

As I look around at the hills and cliffs and seas that God has made, I am overwhelmed by God's goodness. The beauty of creation calls my soul back to life. I resonate with the end of Psalm 42, "Why are you cast down, O my soul, and why are you disquieted within me? Hope in God; for I shall again praise him, my help and my God."

CHAPTER 17

PSALM 119:105–114

105 Your word is a lamp to my feet
and a light to my path.
106 I have sworn an oath and confirmed it,
to observe your righteous ordinances.
107 I am severely afflicted;
give me life, O LORD, according to your word.
108 Accept my offerings of praise, O LORD,
and teach me your ordinances.
109 I hold my life in my hand continually,
but I do not forget your law.
110 The wicked have laid a snare for me,
but I do not stray from your precepts.
111 Your decrees are my heritage forever;
they are the joy of my heart.
112 I incline my heart to perform your statutes
forever, to the end.

113 I hate the double-minded,
but I love your law.
114 You are my hiding place and my shield;
I hope in your word.

LOST SHEEP

LEAVING PORTREE, WE drive north on the Isle of Skye towards our hotel. I hadn't realized we were staying at the very top of the island, but am excited about seeing more of Skye. As we get further away from the city, the road narrows to a one-track lane. Sheep are grazing all around us. Every once in a while we drive over a cattle guard.

"What was that?" my daughter asks after we bump over another grate.

"Oh, that's a cattle guard," answers my farm boy husband. "It keeps the cattle from leaving their farmer's land."

I look out the window at the unfenced moorland around us. "But what keeps them from wandering away if they are not on the road? There doesn't seem to be anything marking the land."

"I don't know," Jason answers. "Maybe it is like the Douglas estate where they mark their sheep with spray paint. Or maybe they have other markers on them?"

I continue to worry about the sheep. They seem to just be walking around as they please. They are grazing by the road, by the sea. What keeps them from getting lost?

Also, what keeps them from getting hit? Camper vans are speeding along this narrow road with no regard for others around them, drivers, pedestrians, or sheep.

No one else seems as concerned about lost sheep. Maybe because the island is not that big. Or maybe because they don't know what it is like to feel well and truly lost. But I do.

Throughout this past year of grief, I have had a profound sense of being unmoored. It is as if whatever rope was connecting me to my anchor has been cut and I am drifting aimlessly in the sea. It has bothered me immensely, this feeling of being lost in the tides. Partly because I did not see this particular side effect of grief coming. I expected to feel sad and tired. I was not surprised at my anger and tendency to isolate. But I never expected to feel so lost.

I did not after all lose my parents while I was still young. Fifty is middle-aged or older by any standard. And while my parents and I were close, we didn't have the kind of relationship where I called them often seeking advice. If anything, our roles were reversed these past few years and I was the one giving advice and help. Why did losing them, Mom in particular make me feel so adrift?

But then I think about how I came into the world attached to my mom by a cord and it makes more sense. Even if I didn't talk to Mom every day or consider her my best friend, she was always there for me. I was a daughter who had a mom in the world. Even if I didn't call her for help with my problems regularly, she was there if I needed her. And being her daughter in the world helped define me. I was Marie's girl. Whether I built upon her life choices or tore them down, she was the foundation for who I became.

And now without her, I don't quite know what to do.

One of the first thoughts that pops into my head after awakening in the morning is, "My mom is gone, I don't have a mom."

I do my best to get up and get on with my day. But inevitably there comes a point where I walk around the room wondering, "What was I just doing? I don't know what to do next." Sometimes I brush this feeling off as a middle-aged moment. But sometimes it goes deeper. There are times when I sit with my head in my hands and feel the profound absence of my mom. The north on a compass I didn't know I had. And without her on this earth, I seem doomed to wander it with no sense of my bearings.

When we get to the hotel, I walk down to the shore. The kids have gone ahead of me since I am taking my time. As I wind through the grass I come upon some sheep. Doubting the hotel owns its own flock, I guess this group has drifted over from somewhere else. They don't seem concerned about being off their homeland. And they appear to have enough sense not to walk too close to the drop-off to the sea. They are just standing and eating the grass and baaing into the wind.

Why can't I be this calm about being lost, I wonder. What do they have that I don't?

And then lines from Psalm 119 come to me, "Thy word is a lamp unto my feet and a light unto my path." These sheep trust their shepherd. They know that even though their shepherd is not standing right beside them, she is near. When they wander too far, she still knows where they are and will safely guide them home. They are not lost because their shepherd has them in her care.

Even though I know God is with me, do I trust Him completely in this time of disorientation? Do I know without a doubt that God has an eye on me and will shine a light for me to follow if I stray too far? Honestly, I don't know. There is so much I don't know right now. My world has been shattered and I am putting it back together piece by piece. Since God's lamp is only lighting my path a step at a time, I still feel lost. How can I re-learn to trust God's hand to guide me?

After making it to the shore and back, I decide to take a nap before dinner. Since the weather is so nice, we open the window to let in the sea breeze. As I drift in and out of sleep, I can hear the sheep gently bleating in the distance. These lines of the Psalm flit through my mind, "you are my hiding place and my shield. I hope in your word." I don't have to worry about being lost in my grief, for God has me. Even when I don't feel it, God is holding me and shielding me. I can't accidentally wander away from God's care. I just have to remember to trust the bit of light I can see and follow it home. With this knowledge settling over me, I fall back asleep.

CHAPTER 18

PSALM 31:1–16, 23–24

1 In you, O LORD, I seek refuge;
do not let me ever be put to shame;
in your righteousness deliver me.
2 Incline your ear to me;
rescue me speedily.
Be a rock of refuge for me,
a strong fortress to save me.

3 You are indeed my rock and my fortress;
for your name's sake lead me and guide me;
4 take me out of the net that is hidden for me,
for you are my refuge.
5 Into your hand I commit my spirit;
you have redeemed me, O LORD, faithful God.

6 You hate those who pay regard to worthless idols,
but I trust in the LORD.
7 I will exult and rejoice in your steadfast love,
because you have seen my affliction;
you have taken notice of my adversities
8 and have not delivered me into the hand of the enemy;
you have set my feet in a broad place.

9 Be gracious to me, O LORD, for I am in distress;
my eye wastes away from grief,
my soul and body also.
10 For my life is spent with sorrow
and my years with sighing;
my strength fails because of my misery,
and my bones waste away.

11 I am the scorn of all my adversaries,
a horror to my neighbors,
an object of dread to my acquaintances;
those who see me in the street flee from me.
12 I have passed out of mind like one who is dead;
I have become like a broken vessel.
13 For I hear the whispering of many—
terror all around!—
as they scheme together against me,
as they plot to take my life.

14 But I trust in you, O LORD;
I say, "You are my God."
15 My times are in your hand;
deliver me from the hand of my enemies and persecutors.
16 Let your face shine upon your servant;
save me in your unfailing love.

23 Love the LORD, all you his saints.
The LORD preserves the faithful
but abundantly repays the one who acts haughtily.
24 Be strong, and let your heart take courage,
all you who wait for the LORD.

CRAGS

AS WE REACH the top of the next rise, I remove my backpack and lean against a boulder to rest. Drinking my water, I look at the landscape around us. Green as far as the eye can see. But grey too, for out of the peat bog rises rocks of various shapes and sizes. The verdancy of Scotland I was expecting, but the plate tectonic explosion of rock everywhere is a surprise. I let my eyes take in the beautiful landscape a little longer before replacing my water bottle in my backpack and climbing towards the upper part of the Fairy Pool Trail.

The trail gets smaller and less predictable. I find my foothold on water-smoothed rocks as we ford a small stream. My husband leads the way as I huff and puff at his back. When the trail steepness increases beyond my legs' strength, I reach out for support. A well-placed stone rising from the ground can be a gift when the path gets tough. I give thanks for discovering God's goodness in small things.

At the next bend, I take another break. I knew walking in Scotland would involve elevation and rugged terrain, but my three months of walking the big hill in our neighborhood hadn't prepared me for this supposedly easy trail.

But so much of life is like that, isn't it? My mind wanders back to the purpose behind this trip, to say goodbye to my dad. Even after ten years of increasing dementia and ill health, his death took me by surprise—correction: my mom's death took me by surprise. My dad's immediate decline and passing were pretty much a given once she was gone. Without his wife and primary caregiver, Dad was lost. She had been his rock these last years. Without her, he didn't care to find a new way forward.

But where did that leave me? On the hardest journey of my life. There were so many times during those three months between Mom's passing and Dad joining her that I wondered how I would go on. I was beyond exhausted—and sad and scared and just plain mad. Why did Mom have to die first? Why was I left alone to walk Dad to his death?

There was nothing to do but keep putting one foot in front of the other. And pray.

Since I am a campus minister, I do a lot of praying. Even when I can't muster the words to intercede for myself, I pray with my students twice weekly at our evening services. We offer the same devotion every time we gather: The Service of Compline from the Book of Common Prayer. The Episcopalians might not be much for spontaneity, but our rituals speak to me always. When we say aloud the words of Psalm 31, *"In You O LORD have I taken refuge, let me never be put to shame, deliver me in your righteousness... Be my strong rock, a castle to keep me safe, for you are my crag and my stronghold,"* I can feel these words coming to life in me.

Praying those words week after week became a lifeline. I drew deeper into the Psalms. "In You, O LORD, I take refuge. Deliver me." I lifted those words to God as if they could save me from this terrible trial. But week after week the trial went on.

Scrambling for hope, I came up with new ways for us to enter the Psalm. We would journal it and meditate on it. One week we even watercolored it. When it was time to paint Psalm 31, I realized I didn't know what a crag was. I had sketched my strong rock on the page beside my castle, but what was a crag? Was it a hole in the rock like a cave? Was it a shelter where I could hide? A safe hiding place would be welcome about now. I googled crag and searched for images. What I found was disappointing. It turns out a crag is a piece of rock jutting up from the ground. There would be no disappearing from my troubles into a crag.

As I stand on the Isle of Skye, it is as if we have landed in the middle of the Psalm. I know the Psalmist was talking about the mountains and hills in Israel's highlands, but the images translate amazingly well. Scotland has plenty of castles (or towers depending on your translation). The highlands are covered with strong rocks. And the crashing of landmasses long ago has assured there are crags. I try to imagine the pressure and conflict that led to this many rocks jutting this far out of the earth. It makes the pressure I was under caring for my dad seem small.

I wonder how many meters are left in this "easy" trail. I debate whether or not I can make it to the top. Lord knows I am so tired of walking hard paths. So tired of being tired. But sometimes the trail (and trial) does go on and on. There are times when there is no place to rest. In those moments all we can pray for is a crag to jut out of the earth and give us something to grab onto as we continue climbing up the path before us.

There were so many days when I thought I would

collapse and die before my dad did. Days when I felt the hardship would be more than I could handle. But I kept walking. Kept praying. And God kept sending me strong rocks to lean on while I caught my breath and crags to grab hold of when the way got rough.

I made it to the end with Dad. I sat by his bedside and wiped his forehead with cool cloths as God guided him to the great beyond.

But here in Scotland, I stop just before the end of the trail. A particularly supportive boulder calls to me and I rest on it. I sit looking beyond my perch to where my husband walks on, to the cleft in the rock. From my point of safety, I observe the fog rolling in and marvel at the mysteries of life and death. I ponder how we never know what is in front of us. We don't know how long the path is or what is around the bend. All we can count on is that God is with us, leading and guiding us. When the way gets hard, we will be given a strong crag to hold onto and God will give us strength to go on.

CHAPTER 19

PSALM 25:1–6, 12–21

1 In you, LORD my God,
I put my trust.
2 I trust in you;
do not let me be put to shame,
nor let my enemies triumph over me.
3 No one who hopes in you
will ever be put to shame,
but shame will come on those
who are treacherous without cause.

4 Show me your ways, LORD,
teach me your paths.
5 Guide me in your truth and teach me,
for you are God my Savior,
and my hope is in you all day long.
6 Remember, LORD, your great mercy and love,
for they are from of old.

12 Who, then, are those who fear the LORD?
He will instruct them in the ways they should choose.
13 They will spend their days in prosperity,

and their descendants will inherit the land.
14 The Lord confides in those who fear him.
He makes his covenant known to them.
15 My eyes are ever on the LORD,
for only he will release my feet from the snare.
16 Turn to me and be gracious to me,
for I am lonely and afflicted.
17 Relieve the troubles of my heart
and free me from my anguish.
18 Look on my affliction and my distress
and take away all my sins.
19 See how numerous are my enemies
and how fiercely they hate me!

20 Guard my life and rescue me;
do not let me be put to shame,
for I take refuge in you.
21 May integrity and uprightness protect me,
because my hope, LORD, is in you.

CLEAVED

THE WAVES LAP gently at the base of Kilt Rock. Their smallness gives perspective to the sheer 90-meter drop from the top to the sea. I am grateful for the chain link fence holding us back from the edge. I don't like heights, and seeing just how far above the water we are unnerves me. I can't help thinking about what it would be like to fall from this great height. I focus instead on the wave-like patterns in the rock that give this geological formation its common name.

My guidebook highly recommended stopping at the Kilt Rock viewing point on the Isle of Skye. The main draw, of course, is the dramatic cliffs framed by Mealt Falls. But there is more here than the breathtaking view. I turn my back to the blowing wind as I read about the geological history that played out here on the Trotternish Peninsula.

The informative plaques paint a picture of a Jurassic age filled with dinosaurs, lava flows, and tectonic drama. The weight of the lava flows, combined with the softness of the basalt, led to massive landslides and even landslips. Large areas of land were cleaved from one another, leaving rocks once attached to vast stretches of earth now standing alone.

This phenomenon led to some astonishing results. Some visitors come to Skye just to see these ancient formations. The Old Man of Storr and the Quiraing have been overrun with tourists every time we have driven by. But as I stare at Kilt Rock again, I wonder what those moments of movement must have been like. What was it like to have part of the land ripped from the rest, leaving a whole ocean between them?

To me, it feels like it would have torn painfully.

That was one of the things I feared most about my parents' deaths: the moment of separation. When you've always been attached to something—grounded by it, even—you cannot imagine its absence. What will it feel like to have your anchor torn away?

In the days leading up to both their deaths, I was grateful to be busy. The hospice nurses were wonderful, but their job was mainly to help our family care for Mom and Dad ourselves. And that care became all-consuming. Even with CNAs and family around, the final weeks of each parent's life were filled with care tasks, visitors, and making plans.

When friends called to check on me, I reassured them I was in Steel Magnolia mode. Honestly, I was leaning into it harder than necessary. As a Southern woman, planning and caretaking are well-worn, comforting activities for me. But I knew there would come a moment all my planning and caregiving hadn't prepared me for.

The moment of letting go.

When it finally came, the moment was easier than I feared. A mix of my exhaustion and the nature of their death allowed me to release my grip a little. Like childbirth, a slow, natural death takes its own course. At some point, I knew Someone else was so in control of this moment that I didn't have to be.

And then they were gone.

Again, I slipped back into planning mode to ease my grief. There were family members to call and arrangements to make. It wasn't until well after the funerals that I truly felt my parents' absence. At first, it felt like they weren't completely gone—more like they'd gone away on a trip but hadn't fully left my sphere of existence. It seemed they were out there, just out of reach.

And as time wore on, the sense of absence grew. It began to sink in that I'd lost a part of myself. Some bits of me were gone and weren't coming back. At first, I wasn't sure how to go on with part of me gone forever. How do I live now that I am alone—cleaved from the woman who bore me, separated from the man who raised me? They had shaped me into who I am, how could I continue without them?

But that was exactly what I had to learn. I had to walk this earth on my own two feet from now on. Like the Old Man of Storr, I had to learn to stand strong after the landslide passed.

In my loneliness, I turned to God. I prayed to the One who would never let me walk alone. I called out with the Psalmist, "In you, LORD my God, I put my trust. Show me your ways LORD, teach me your paths." If I was going to find my way in this new life, God would have to show me the path forward.

At first, it felt like baby steps. I felt like I was relearning how to walk in a world without my parents. Then my walk became more confident, more sure. On days when I felt uncertain, I reminded myself, "Your word is a lamp to my feet and a light to my path." I didn't need to see the whole way forward; I only needed to take the next step.

When I look at Kilt Rock again, it seems brave, abiding there on the edge of the coast. Like it's holding back the sea from the rest of the land and keeping the earth from falling into the water. How long will I have to practice living on my own before I feel that strong and brave?

It doesn't really matter, I guess. What I need to focus on now is walking back to the car and getting ready for dinner. Then, waking up and starting a new day. It doesn't do me well to get ahead of myself. I'll keep taking one step after another, trusting God to light my path as I go and direct my ways. Time will take care of itself.

CHAPTER 20

Psalm 46

1 God is our refuge and strength,
an ever-present help in trouble.
2 Therefore we will not fear, though the earth give way
and the mountains fall into the heart of the sea,
3 though its waters roar and foam
and the mountains quake with their surging.

4 There is a river whose streams
make glad the city of God,
the holy place where the Most High dwells.
5 God is within her, she will not fall;
God will help her at break of day.
6 Nations are in uproar, kingdoms fall;
he lifts his voice, the earth melts.

7 The LORD Almighty is with us;
the God of Jacob is our fortress.

8 Come and see what the LORD has done,
the desolations he has brought on the earth.
9 He makes wars cease

to the ends of the earth.
He breaks the bow and shatters the spear;
he burns the shields with fire.
10 He says, "Be still, and know that I am God;
I will be exalted among the nations,
I will be exalted in the earth."

11 The LORD Almighty is with us;
the God of Jacob is our fortress.

PEAT

JASON MOVES OVER to make room for me as we find a place to stand in Talisker's education room. On this first stop of our distillery tour, we are to learn the basics of Scottish whisky making. "I am not sure I am going to like whisky," our daughter worries.

"No matter. It will be fun to learn more about it while we are here," I reassure. Scotch whisky making is an old and famous tradition in Scotland. Visiting one of Scotland's 150 distilleries will help us learn more about the land and its people.

The tour guide begins to explain the basic steps of making whisky here in this almost 200-year-old establishment. We learn words like mash and malt. Then she begins to describe what makes Talisker Scotch different. The company was built by the shore near freshwater springs. Because the makers want their whisky to have a peaty profile, they run the spring water through peat on the way into the facility. Then they burn peat while the whisky is malting.

While our guide talks on, my gaze drifts over to the illustration of peat on the wall. I know what peat is, as I have read my fair share of British historical romances. It is a partially composted plant matter that exists for multiple feet below the ground's surface. Historically, people dug it up in small bricks that they burned in the fireplace for heat.

I refocus to hear the guide explain how this peaty profile ties their whisky to the land of Scotland and its people. The peatlands of the Scottish Highlands are an iconic part of the culture here. I wonder if the burning peat smells like a cold, wet Scottish day.

As we walk through the different rooms where the whisky is made, I keep coming back to the peat. Of all the land features in Scotland, peat bogs are among the least dramatic. How can something so everyday as the slow composting of plants in wet soil be more powerful than a tectonic rift? What kind of transformation must a dead plant go through to become such a valuable commodity? What must it feel like to endure a thousand years of pressure so that you can be transformed?

We all know what pressure feels like. These past two years have definitely been a pressure cooker for our family. We all took on extra responsibilities as my mom and dad declined in health. First I started managing all their medications. Then, my brother took over all their bills. Then I began accompanying Mom to the grocery store. Then I went to the store alone.

As more and more responsibility fell on my shoulders, I felt weighed down. My mind was continually full of the list of things I needed to do for my parents. I feared getting sick, not for my own sake, but because I worried about how my own illness would leave my parents in the lurch.

The pressure increased until I was wound as tight as could be.

People began to worry about me. Friends encouraged me to put my parents in a residential facility. My therapist encouraged me to set boundaries. Their advice was all well and good, but the thing about walking through the Valley of the Shadow of Death is we all have to walk it in our own way.

I knew my parents wanted to stay at home as long as possible (and even when it seemed impossible). They had been adamant about it. And whereas boundaries are all well and good, if I didn't do some of these things for my parents, who would? We did hire a helper for Mom and Dad. As they worsened, we steadily increased her hours. But at the end of the day, even she could only do so much. And some forms of care they only wanted from me. And part of me needed to give it to them.

That is the thing about losing your elderly parents. At some point you know they are dying. That you only have so many more trips to the grocery store before they are gone. If refilling their medicine organizers one more time was how I could show my love, then that was what I would do. They were small everyday tasks, but suddenly they felt sacred.

As the pressure continued to weigh down on me, I wondered what would be left of me when my parents were gone. It felt like everything had fallen apart—and was still falling. My energy was gone, my joy thinning. I felt like a shell of my former self.

Then we entered the last stretch with my mom, and I stopped paying attention to myself. All I could think about was holding her up until it was time to hand her over to God. The hospice nurses taught me how to administer morphine and give Mom a sponge bath. Mom's caregiver and I became an ace team—turning her, cleaning her, giving her the same care she gave me as a baby. My brother and I took turns being close until she took her last turn.

As we entered the small hours of the morning Mom would die, the pressure finally lifted. I knew she was going to be free. And somehow I sensed part of me would be freed as well. I would no longer have to worry about her struggling or suffering. God would have her. She would be okay.

In those last moments as Mom slipped away from us, something inside me loosened. All the love I had been pouring into her these past years was released—not lost, but freed. It was lifted out of my grave of worry and fear and allowed to rest with her as she rose into God's care with the dawn. All that love was not lost but transformed into something new and beautiful. A final gift, warming my heart even after Mom left this earth. I sat in stillness before God, awed by the mystery of it.

I was reminded of chemist Antoine Lavoisier's words, "nothing is wasted—everything is transformed."

After we leave the distillery, I stare out the window at the peat bogs stretching across the landscape. It is strange how a dead plant, lying half-decomposed in soupy soil, can transform into the fuel that warms a nation. How something pressed down for centuries can come to define a people so deeply they want their favorite drink to smell and taste like it.

But I understand. I know the love and loss of my parents will mark me for the rest of my life, and I wouldn't really want it any other way. But instead of leaving me hollowed out, walking with them through their deaths changed me into a person of deep warmth and love. God was my strength through that long, hard process. I don't understand the mystery of God's handiwork, but I give thanks that nothing, not even grief and loss is wasted. Somehow, in God's hands, it can all be redeemed.

CHAPTER 21

PSALM 13

1 How long, O LORD? Will you forget me forever?
How long will you hide your face from me?
2 How long must I bear pain in my soul
and have sorrow in my heart all day long?
How long shall my enemy be exalted over me?

3 Consider and answer me, O LORD my God!
Give light to my eyes, or I will sleep the sleep of death,
4 and my enemy will say, "I have prevailed";
my foes will rejoice because I am shaken.

5 But I trusted in your steadfast love;
my heart shall rejoice in your salvation.
6 I will sing to the LORD
because he has dealt bountifully with me.

HOW LONG

ACROSS THE HIGHWAY from where we've pulled over, I spot an old crofter's house nestled against a hill. I noticed several of these on our drive along the A890 from Skye towards Inverness. This highway, stretching across the base of the Highlands, seems to reflect the everyday history of the area more than some of the more touristy places we have visited.

As Jason and the kids take pictures of the loch in the valley below, I keep looking back at that cottage and trying to imagine the life inside it—the kind of life that asks you to stay put when the world is shifting under your feet. Crofting—small farming on a sliver of land—became more common after the Highland Clearances in the 1800s. Before that, farmers lived and worked together on shared family land.

During the clearances, previously open land was fenced, and rent was raised, leaving farmers with less land and fewer options. Their hard lives were made even harder by the potato famine of the mid-1800s. During these years, survival as a farmer in the Scottish Highlands became nearly impossible. As a result, almost a third of

Highland farmers emigrated. But this house belonged to someone who stayed. Someone who waited out the famine and whatever backlash came afterward, and still tried to build a life after the suffering they endured.

But waiting out the hard times can take longer than you think you can bear.

I've never lived through a famine, but I have lived through a season that felt endless. We began to suspect Dad had dementia in his late seventies. He forgot names and events, and then he began to say and do things that were out of character. When he could no longer manage tasks he had always done well, we knew something was wrong.

So, Mom and I went with him to the doctor for help. I don't know whether the doctor was dismissive to appease my father—who was furious at my accusations of memory loss—or because he already knew there was nothing to be done. Instead of prescribing a memory medication, he handed me a copy of *The 36-Hour Day.*

Every time I read a few pages, I wanted to throw that book against a wall. I didn't want to learn how to care for a parent with dementia—possibly Alzheimer's. I was only forty. I wanted my dad back.

After repeated calls and emails to Dad's doctor, we finally got a referral to a neurologist. The specialist went over my father's scans with us, and the diagnosis became clear—vascular dementia.

Years of poorly controlled blood pressure had taken their toll on Dad's brain. The neurologist showed us the damage on the scan—stiffened blood vessels and withered tissue that led to Dad's persistent confusion. There is no cure for vascular dementia. There is only coping.

Because Dad was still in decent physical health, we

started learning how to support him—how to live with these limitations for what could be years. Mom began driving whenever they went anywhere together. When we ran into old friends at dinner, I'd introduce myself first and ask them to remind me of their name, so Dad wouldn't have to stumble. My brother helped Mom organize the finances and automate bills.

The hardest parts came in fresh waves—each time Dad lost another ability. After he bungled a tax return one year, we had to tell friends he could no longer be their tax advisor. Even in retirement, he'd worked part-time for a tax company. And he was so good at it he did most of his friends' taxes for free. But not anymore. I still don't know who that admission hurt most—Dad, embarrassed by his confusion; his friends, losing a piece of their buddy; or Mom, having to admit her husband was fading right in front of her.

And then there was the everyday drip of hardships: trying to prevent Dad from driving himself places, navigating his frustration when he couldn't remember how to do something, and managing my own frustration when he couldn't remember details about my life.

Strangely, our kids handled it better than anyone. They simply met their grandaddy where he was. Since their relationship was glued together with TV time and snacks, they leaned into this rhythm, keeping them his rock-solid favorites.

But I crumbled. My father was one of the smartest, most capable men I had ever known. As mad as I could get at him, I trusted him to be himself—a sometimes infuriating but always loving presence in my life. As he began to shift and change, I felt my own foundation begin to rock.

One of the frustrating things about dementia is you don't know how it is going to play out. Some people decline rapidly and die within a couple of years. Others decline slowly and live much longer. Dad seemed to decline in spurts and then ride plateaus for long periods of time. I began to try to enjoy those plateaus.

But still, at night I found myself wiping tears and asking God: how long? How long would I have to watch Dad decline? How long would I live with the pain and anger and sadness of watching my dad suffer, and then die?

There was no clear answer. Dad would suffer a setback, then stabilize. When he broke his hip, I thought surely this was it. But after six weeks in rehab, he came home with a walker. At some point, I began to wonder if he would outlive us all.

As it turned out, he did outlive Mom. After caring for her husband for twelve years, Mom's own health began to decline. After a sharp turn with kidney disease, she outran him to heaven.

I will never know who was angrier when Mom died first, me or Dad. We were both heartbroken and furious. He wailed while I held his hand and repeated, "I know, I know." How could we ever survive this new blow?

But for three months, we did. Dad's caregivers were a constant, loving presence in his life. I was a daily visitor who held his hand and made him laugh. As for me, I just kept putting one foot in front of the other.

The answer to how long I could hold the pain of caring for my declining Dad turned out to be this: way longer than I thought was humanly possible. People told me I was strong, which only served to anger me. Couldn't they see the only reason I appeared strong was because I had been carrying a heavy burden for so long?

I began to recognize this same trait in others. I would clock them walking around with coffee cups in their hands, dark circles under their eyes, shoulders hunched forward. We were the people doing what had to be done. The burden bearers.

At some point I stopped resenting my burden. My husband Jason would always commiserate, "It is what it is." I didn't like that phrase, I preferred, "It is what we choose it to be." And at some point, I chose to take care of my dad until God welcomed him home.

My spiritual director helped me get to this point. We talked about how compassion is a Latin word that means "suffering with". I chose to enter Dad's journey of suffering with him willingly—to accept both the pain and the unexpected blessings the road had to offer. The rocky path wounded me often, but somehow, God always filled and bound those wounds up with love.

Dad finally died a few weeks after turning ninety. We held vigil at his bedside for almost a week. Even in the last moments of death, he was slower in leaving than Mom. I went home around eight that final evening, knowing he probably wouldn't last until morning. But after twelve long years and three hard months of caring for him, I felt at peace. I had said everything I needed to say and done everything I had to do. God had him now. I asked my brother to call me after Dad took his last breath.

When I got the call around four in the morning that my father was dead, I thanked God. The battle was over, and we had all made it—even Dad. I was so grateful he was finally free of suffering and reunited with Mom. He was finally free.

After twelve years and three excruciating months, he was free.

The answer to "How long, O LORD?" is, sadly, as long as it takes. We often have no idea how long that will be. For the farmers in Scotland and Ireland, the potato blight lasted for ten years. Somehow, some way, by the grace of God, most of us find a way to make it through. We make it through tired and wounded, but full of God's love. Always full of God's love.

CHAPTER 22

PSALM 74:1–17, 21

1 O God, why do you cast us off forever?
Why does your anger smoke against
the sheep of your pasture?
2 Remember your congregation,
which you acquired long ago,
which you redeemed to be the tribe of your heritage.
Remember Mount Zion, where you came to dwell.
3 Direct your steps to the perpetual ruins;
the enemy has destroyed everything in the sanctuary.

4 Your foes have roared within your holy place;
they set up their emblems there.
5 At the upper entrance they hacked
the wooden trellis with axes.
6 And then, with hatchets and hammers,
they smashed all its carved work.
7 They set your sanctuary on fire;
they desecrated the dwelling place of your name,
bringing it to the ground.
8 They said to themselves, "We will utterly subdue them";
they burned all the meeting places of God in the land.

12 Yet God my King is from of old,
working salvation in the earth.
13 You divided the sea by your might;
you broke the heads of the dragons in the waters.
14 You crushed the heads of Leviathan;
you gave him as food for the creatures of the wilderness.
15 You cut openings for springs and torrents;
you dried up ever-flowing streams.
16 Yours is the day, yours also the night;
you established the luminaries and the sun.
17 You have fixed all the bounds of the earth;
you made summer and winter.

21 Do not let the downtrodden be put to shame;
let the poor and needy praise your name.

SEA MONSTERS

MY CHILDREN AND I smile and snicker as the boat heads out onto Loch Ness. This loch cruise will be different from our nature and history-oriented tour of Loch Lomond. Instead of castles and mountains, today we are focused on sea monsters.

I don't know if it is because we are silly-tired a week into our vacation or because we love a legend. For whatever reason, we have decided to go all in on Nessie. My kids took pictures with the large, ceramic Nessie in the parking lot and bought stuffed Nessies in the gift shop. We can't get enough of the long-necked green legend.

When a voice comes over the loudspeaker telling us the sonar is scanning for movement beneath the water and to keep our eyes peeled across the waves, I find myself looking. As much as we have made fun of the myth of the Loch Ness monster this last week, a part of me wants to believe.

I will tell my family it is because I hold open the possibility for mystery. After all, who knows if the descendant of a dinosaur lives in a very remote, very deep Scottish lake? But in truth the real reason is different. Sea monsters and I go back a ways.

I first became fascinated with sea monsters in seminary. In my Old Testament class, my professor explained how the ancient Israelites viewed the seas. The Hebrew word used to describe large bodies of water, Tehom, didn't just refer to the size of the water. It was used to convey a primordial deep that was full of chaos and danger—and sea monsters.

When the Spirit of God moves across the formless deep in Genesis chapter one, bringing light and separating the oceans from land and sky from sea, this is not just organization. These actions show God taming a chaotic and destructive force. And when God breaks the head of the monsters in the water and crushes the Leviathan in Psalm 74, this is a reminder that no chaotic danger in this world is a match for God's mighty power and tender care for us.

This taming of the monster of the deep has resonated with me throughout my life. For there have been times when I was eye to eye with the threat and danger of chaos. One of these times was when my dad struggled with dementia.

When Dad was diagnosed with dementia at age 80, we were told it was a terminal illness. The only question was how long the dementia would take to kill him. This threat loomed over me night and day. Would Dad decline quickly? Would it be better if he went fast? Would he suffer for years on end? How bad would his mind get before he died? The serpent of worry wound its way around my mind until I was choked with fear.

I knew I had no control over how Dad's disease and eventual death would play out. What I had to remind myself over and over again was that God did.

I would read my favorite Scriptures repeatedly to

remind myself that our God is the God who tames the waters of chaos at creation and in my life today. Ours is the God who put the bow in the sky after taming the dangerous waters of the flood and who would not let me drown in the waters of this hardship. Our God tames the sea serpent Leviathan and can tame the serpent of fear in my mind.

In the end, Dad struggled with dementia for ten years. In some ways, those years were long and grueling. In others, they were a gift. Though Dad's vascular dementia progressed slowly over time, he never lost the ability to recognize family and friends. He always knew he was at home with people he loved. In his confusion, he might fight with us for days on end and accuse us of plotting against him, but deep down he knew he loved us and we loved him.

Though sometimes the waters of chaos lapped against me and the deadly sea serpent seemed to swim around my waist, I was never taken under during my time of trial. Moreover, I knew I was never alone. God was walking with me through these waters, giving me the strength to keep going through a hard and scary time.

Maybe this is why I am not afraid of the Loch Ness monster even though part of me believes it is real. Even if a primordial sea monster is swimming below me, it is still subject to God, the creator of the universe. Even if I can't explain it, I know God can.

At the end of my time with Dad when things became arduous, I asked God the unanswerable question. Why? Why did Mom have to die before Dad? Why was I left to care for him alone? During these times of questioning, I would turn to the Book of Job. When Job asks God the unanswerable question about his suffering, God responds with a four-chapter long blast beginning with, "Where were you when I laid the foundations of the earth?" God goes on to talk about the creation and subjugation of the world, asking Job if he too can play with Leviathan like a pet.

As I stare out to where the mountains meet the clouds, this is where my thoughts end up. I don't have to know all the whys or hows or even ifs. Is there a Loch Ness monster? I don't know. All I know is God is beside me here in these placid waters and any other waters I end up in. I will not be overtaken by them or any monster within. And today, that is enough.

CHAPTER 23

PSALM 139:1–14, 17–18

1 O LORD, you have searched me and known me.
2 You know when I sit down and when I rise up;
you discern my thoughts from far away.
3 You search out my path and my lying down
and are acquainted with all my ways.
4 Even before a word is on my tongue,
O LORD, you know it completely.
5 You hem me in, behind and before,
and lay your hand upon me.
6 Such knowledge is too wonderful for me;
it is so high that I cannot attain it.

7 Where can I go from your spirit?
Or where can I flee from your presence?
8 If I ascend to heaven, you are there;
if I make my bed in Sheol, you are there.
9 If I take the wings of the morning
and settle at the farthest limits of the sea,
10 even there your hand shall lead me,
and your right hand shall hold me fast.
11 If I say, "Surely the darkness shall cover me,

and night wraps itself around me,"
12 even the darkness is not dark to you;
the night is as bright as the day,
for darkness is as light to you.

13 For it was you who formed my inward parts;
you knit me together in my mother's womb.
14 I praise you, for I am fearfully and wonderfully made.

17 How weighty to me are your thoughts, O God!
How vast is the sum of them!
18 I try to count them—they are more than the sand;
I come to the end—I am still with you.

HAUNTED

I STARE AT THE old woman in the portrait hanging across from the reception desk as Jason checks our family into Bunchrew House. The most historic of all the places we will stay, this baronial mansion leans into its 400-year-old history with paintings of family members scattered throughout the main floor. "Well, I think this house definitely wins the most likely to be haunted award," I say to Jason as we pick up our bags and head to our room. I steal one last glance at the woman. Her dour, worn face is hooded by a black cape swathed around her head and shoulders. "I really don't want to run into her on the way to the bathroom in the middle of the night."

"Yeah, I read that it was built in the 1600s and was passed from family member to family member for hundreds of years before it was sold to be a hotel. Crazy to imagine, huh?" Jason uses an actual key to let us into our room. "If I had a house as nice as this one, I guess I would try and hold onto it too."

After we settle in, we climb down one half of our staircase and then turn at a landing to go down a hall to the kids' room. "Sure is a big, winding place, isn't it?" Jason asks. He knocks on the door.

As Eli lets us in, Libby looks up from her bed. "Tell me a ghost is not going to get me in the middle of the night." Jason laughs and reassures her. I don't feel quite as confident. This place is old and steeped in family history. Most likely to be haunted indeed.

Down in the drawing room before dinner, I walk over to a large portrait of a beautiful young woman. She is pictured standing, wearing a formal, floor-length gown. Having few pictures and zero paintings of my ancestors, I wonder what it would be like to stare at their images every day. Would I be comforted or disturbed? What must it be like having your dead family members around you all the time?

Even as I ask this question, I know the answer. Bittersweet.

In the weeks after each parent's death, I could still feel their presence near me. Whether this was because they were with me in some metaphysical sense or whether there were ripples of their presence lingering around me, I will never know. I just know I never really felt apart from them.

As time went on and I began to heal, I wished I could feel my dead parents a little less. If I wasn't reminded of them so often, maybe I would feel less sad. Forgetting about them for just one day might help the grief and pain fade too. But they were everywhere I looked. They were in the inherited furniture now in my house. They were at the grocery store when I saw Mom's favorite salad kits or Dad's favorite candy bars. Reminders of my folks haunted me all around.

And then slowly, I began to forget. I'd make it through the grocery store without tearing up. I'd polish the dining room table without thinking of our family meals together. The memory of my parents began fading from my life. And then I realized, I didn't want to stop being haunted by them. Because if I was, I might forget them entirely. How could I live if I couldn't remember Dad's melodious baritone voice or the color of Mom's eyes?

I can only do so much to remember my parents. I have their photos hanging in my house and happy reminders of our life together around me. The dining table, the piano, Dad's watch, Mom's jewelry. The items bring them a little closer to me when I miss them most.

But in the end, I can't cling to them. I was never meant to. As Isaiah tells us, people are impermanent—only God is eternal. God is the one rock I can hold onto that will never fade or fail. For even before I was my parents' child, I was God's. God was with me before I was born and is with me after my parents' death.

This may be the one haunting I am okay with. "Where can I go from your Spirit? Where can I flee from your presence… If I take the wings of the morning and settle at the farthest limits of the sea, even there your hand shall lead me, and your right hand shall hold me fast." Yes, please. Let me be inescapable from God's presence. Let me never outrun the goodness of the Lord, my God.

I cannot forget God, because God will not let me. Yet, God also does not leave Mom. Nor does God leave Dad.

As we are called into dinner, this thought comforts me. Though I do not understand the mysteries of heaven and earth, I know God is above and among it all. God holds my parents. And God holds me. And somehow in that mystery we are still connected. The communion of the saints surrounds us all the time. I say goodbye to the lady in the portrait knowing that even she is held in the immeasurable wonder of God's grace.

CHAPTER 24

PSALM 103:1–5, 10–18

1 Bless the LORD, O my soul,
and all that is within me,
bless his holy name.
2 Bless the LORD, O my soul,
and do not forget all his benefits—
3 who forgives all your iniquity,
who heals all your diseases,
4 who redeems your life from the Pit,
who crowns you with steadfast love and mercy,
5 who satisfies you with good as long as you live
so that your youth is renewed like the eagle's.

10 He does not deal with us according to our sins
nor repay us according to our iniquities.
11 For as the heavens are high above the earth,
so great is his steadfast love toward those who fear him;
12 as far as the east is from the west,
so far he removes our transgressions from us.
13 As a father has compassion for his children,
so the Lord has compassion for those who fear him.
14 For he knows how we were made;

he remembers that we are dust.

15 As for mortals, their days are like grass;
they flourish like a flower of the field;
16 for the wind passes over it, and it is gone,
and its place knows it no more.
17 But the steadfast love of the LORD
is from everlasting to everlasting
on those who fear him,
and his righteousness to children's children,
18 to those who keep his covenant
and remember to do his commandments.

GOOD ENOUGH

WE WALK DOWN the street looking for an open restaurant. It is dinner time, and we are getting hungry. I haven't made a reservation for our evening meal and the restaurants we pass are spilling over with people. We are tired, hungry, and don't feel like waiting to be seated.

So my family and I keep walking through the brick-lined streets in the tourist district of Inverness. We notice that many restaurants we walk by will close within the hour. We forgot that places in Scotland tend to close earlier than American establishments. We begin to feel a little desperate.

As we walk by a McDonald's on the corner of two main streets, my son pipes up, "Honestly, I would be okay eating at McDonald's right now. I am tired and just want a little something to eat." We all scan each other's faces for reactions. We don't even eat at McDonald's in America. Jason and I tried to raise our kids to eat healthy food, so we avoided mass-produced fast food if at all possible.

But we are so tired. And desperate times call for desperate measures. "I could go for some McDonald's ice cream," my daughter offers. We joke that hopefully the ice cream machines in Scottish McDonalds work better than those in America.

The next thing we know, we are in line checking out all the McFlurry flavors. One of the fun things about eating at an American chain overseas is seeing how they do things differently. The McFlurry options do not disappoint. "Hmm, Oreo, Malt balls—oh Biscoff. I think I will try Biscoff," I announce.

As we sit at our table quietly enjoying our British ice cream experience, I do not feel in the least bit guilty for having milkshakes for dinner. One of the things I have learned this past year of grieving is that you have to take it easy on yourself. Some of the best advice I got in the early days was "If someone offers to help you, let them." And don't expect too much of yourself for a while. This is a time to take it easy.

Because I work in campus ministry, and Dad died in May, I was able to take a few weeks off after his death to rest and recover from the roller coaster of caring for him for three months without Mom. Then I slowly started to re-engage with my normal life. As the fall semester kicked off, I realized I was still not functioning at one hundred percent. Frustrated, I started to lower my standards for the "year of grief."

At home, Jason pitched in a lot and I found some workarounds. I bought pre-made casseroles from a local store and hired a maid for a while. Sometimes I felt like a failure because I couldn't keep up with my normal pace of life. Then a friend or my therapist would remind me that I was still recovering from one of life's great losses. Though I am notoriously hard on myself most of the time, this was certainly one occasion where I could lean into taking it a little easier. "Give yourself grace" became a life motto.

In this way, my grief taught me an important spiritual lesson. If God knows that I am only human and have compassion for my failings and limitations, then perhaps I can learn to have compassion for myself as well. I don't always have to do my best. Sometimes good enough is good enough.

I still did not always love not being able to function like my pre-grief self, but I began developing kindness towards myself. For if God is a God of loving-kindness, then I should be a person of loving-kindness. And if I can show mercy towards myself, then I can grow in my ability to show mercy to others as well.

As we finish our shakes, I look around at the other people in the restaurant with us. What has brought them to McDonald's at 8 p.m. on a Tuesday? What battles are they fighting that might make their life hard right now? I pray they may be shown kindness in their struggle, if not by others, at least by themselves. And that they would know exactly how much their God loves them, and how much compassion and mercy is being showered on them from above.

As we walk back into the misty evening, I am so grateful for grace. That God has paved the way for me to learn to be gentle with myself and others. May we all feel the softness and ease of Christ's mercy when we need it most.

CHAPTER 25

Psalm 61

1 Hear my cry, O God;
listen to my prayer.
2 From the end of the earth I call to you,
when my heart is faint.

Lead me to the rock
that is higher than I,
3 for you are my refuge,
a strong tower against the enemy.

4 Let me abide in your tent forever,
find refuge under the shelter of your wings.
5 For you, O God, have heard my vows;
you have given me the heritage of
those who fear your name.

6 Prolong the life of the king;
may his years endure to all generations!
7 May he be enthroned forever before God;
appoint steadfast love and faithfulness to watch over him!

8 So I will always sing praises to your name,
as I pay my vows day after day.

STRONG TOWER

WE STRETCH OUR bodies after climbing out of the car in front of Stirling Castle. We all got a little drowsy on the drive down from Blair Castle. The walk up to the entrance of the fortress helps get my blood pumping and revives me from my sleepy state. After walking through the entry gate, we realize we are only in an outer courtyard. We take a couple of selfies in front of the second entryway and then enter the main area of the castle. My son's face comes alive, and he notices we are in a maze of walls, ramparts, and inner buildings made of ancient stone.

We pick up the pace as we start exploring. We climb down into servants' quarters and up into guard lookout posts. We wind our way around and around until we get to the main buildings where the royalty lived. I marvel that this is not so much a castle as a small city, with the king and queen living in the largest and most protected part. When we finally get inside the chambers most used by the royalty living in Stirling, I feel the protection of the many walls and guards that would have stood between outside invaders and those living inside this stronghold. Words from Psalm

61 come to mind, "for you are my refuge, a strong tower against the enemy."

Since I pray Compline multiple times a week, I am more familiar with Psalm 31 and the images of a strong fortress and the rock of refuge. But Mom's pastor clearly talked about God as Mom's strong tower in her funeral sermon. For some reason that image stuck in my mind.

I longed for a strong tower for us in those last years. When attack after attack came against us, Dad's dementia, the pandemic, Mom's dementia diagnosis—it seemed there was no safe place to rest from it all. Arrow after arrow of sickness and suffering sailed at us, more often than not drawing blood. It seemed impossible that we would be able to survive this ongoing onslaught. As we walk towards the great hall, I think how nice it would be to have a strong tower to protect us.

In the great hall, I take lots of pictures of the Douglas windows. During the 1400s, the Douglases were a powerful clan in Scotland. Good Sir James Douglas fought beside Robert the Bruce in wars of independence and was loyal until his dying breath; he was killed while trying to fulfill Bruce's dying wish of having his heart buried in the Holy Land. I feel proud that our Douglas ancestors were brave and highly regarded in Scottish history.

After leaving the hall, we find ourselves in a quiet garden. When I read the placard, I am surprised to learn we are standing in the Douglas Garden. So named because it is where William Douglas, the 8th Earl of Douglas, died after being brutally stabbed by King James II and then thrown out of a tower window into the garden below. I shake my head at the irony of being invited to have dinner with a compatriot, only to be killed. I guess even strong fortresses are not safe when your growing power makes you dangerous to the king.

As my daughter takes my picture in the garden, I think about how often the things we build to protect ourselves end up failing us. In my efforts to protect my parents and myself, I built a lot of what I thought were strong towers—plans, backups, contingencies meant to hold chaos at bay. But none of my parapets were a match for sickness and death.

It turns out there is only one strong tower that does not fail, and that strong tower is not built by me.

I read Scripture and prayed throughout the battle I walked through with my parents. Even so, it took a while for the words of the Psalms to sink in and for me to realize the rock that is higher than I, my refuge and true strong tower in this last battle, was God. Only God could save my parents, could save me.

But those acts of saving grace looked much different than I had originally planned them. Mom and Dad were to leave their earthly bodies and dwell in the heavenly castle, one where they would never cry or suffer or hurt again. And I was to let go of their hands so I could be held in the strong arms of God. This outcome was not what I wanted—my ways are not always God's ways. But eventually, I had to let go of my own will and accept that this was not defeat. We all die. But that is not the end of the story.

As I sit in the garden thinking about life and death, I feel less alone than I had in a while. Mom and Dad's absence on earth left a large hole in my heart. Even so, I am not forsaken. My heavenly parent is with me, guarding me in my grief.

Looking out over the castle walls, I understand

nothing can keep us safe from suffering, pain, and death in this life. But when we commit our spirits to the strong hand of God, we can rest assured that even in the fiercest battle our Redeemer will ultimately save us.

CHAPTER 26

Psalm 77

1 I cried out to God for help;
I cried out to God to hear me.
2 When I was in distress, I sought the LORD;
at night I stretched out untiring hands,
and I would not be comforted.

3 I remembered you, God, and I groaned;
I meditated, and my spirit grew faint.
4 You kept my eyes from closing;
I was too troubled to speak.
5 I thought about the former days,
the years of long ago;
6 I remembered my songs in the night.
My heart meditated and my spirit asked:

7 "Will the LORD reject forever?
Will he never show his favor again?
8 Has his unfailing love vanished forever?
Has his promise failed for all time?
9 Has God forgotten to be merciful?
Has he in anger withheld his compassion?"

10 Then I thought, “To this I will appeal:
the years when the Most High
stretched out his right hand.
11 I will remember the deeds of the LORD;
yes, I will remember your miracles of long ago.
12 I will consider all your works
and meditate on all your mighty deeds.”

13 Your ways, God, are holy.
What god is as great as our God?
14 You are the God who performs miracles;
you display your power among the peoples.
15 With your mighty arm you redeemed your people,
the descendants of Jacob and Joseph.

16 The waters saw you, God,
the waters saw you and writhed;
the very depths were convulsed.
17 The clouds poured down water,
the heavens resounded with thunder;
your arrows flashed back and forth.
18 Your thunder was heard in the whirlwind,
your lightning lit up the world;
the earth trembled and quaked.
19 Your path led through the sea,
your way through the mighty waters,
though your footprints were not seen.

20 You led your people like a flock
by the hand of Moses and Aaron

BROKEN

I SCRUNCH MY FISTS tighter to stop the tears from falling. It is no use. A tear streams down the right side of my face and unleashes the dam of salty sadness that has been stuffed down inside of me. "I don't know what exactly I did wrong," Jason sighs. I can't blame him. I don't know either, though I am furious at him.

We have been fighting for half an hour inside our hotel room. The best I can explain is that I didn't like his tone when he asked me to move out of the way so he could bring the luggage into our room.

It's been a long day. We started in Inverness and visited two castles on the way down to Edinburgh. It hasn't been a bad day. In fact, most would look at us from the outside and say that we had a great day exploring Blair and Stirling Castles. But it has been long, and in some ways, hard.

For today is my birthday, and my parents are dead.

I did not expect today to be so hard—not like last year. My 50th birthday came only three weeks after my dad died. I didn't want a party or a celebration. All I wanted was a card from Jason and Eli and a call from Libby in Copenhagen.

My grief was too fresh, and I was too tired. After Dad's funeral, I collapsed, got sick with a bad cold, and was only just beginning to recover. But in the end, I felt well enough to go out to dinner. I put on my favorite dress and some lip gloss and celebrated the simple fact that I had woken up and greeted a new day for fifty years—not everyone gets this chance.

This year I thought it would be easier. I was in Scotland with my family on my birthday for goodness' sake. What else could I want? It turns out I wanted parents who were alive.

Birthdays were always a big deal growing up. Maybe because I was the surprise baby girl born after years of secondary infertility. Mom and Dad always bought me a cake and balloons and sang the most ridiculous, purposefully off-key rendition of "Happy Birthday" they could manage. I would make a wish and blow out my candles and everyone would cheer.

There would be no phone call to sing me "Happy Birthday" this year. I have a voicemail saved of them singing to me a couple of years ago. Something told me to save it for posterity. Maybe I knew time was getting short. But I can't bring myself to listen to it.

I just feel broken and tired.

This is what I eventually tell Jason when I finally stop crying. It is my 51st birthday, and I feel broken with grief, and I don't know if I will ever feel whole again. I knew in my head that losing my parents would be hard. That I would feel sad. But I couldn't anticipate how I would feel shattered into a million pieces. It has been over a year since Dad died. Shouldn't I be doing better by now?

I know other people think this too. I am sure my family is tired of my moods, and my friends probably wonder why I am not around as much anymore. It's just so hard to do all the things I used to be able to do.

When we both calm down enough, Jason puts his hand on my shoulder and tells me it will be okay. "I am sorry you feel broken. Remember it won't be this bad forever." He rubs my back. "One day you will be put back together again. Life will be different, but you will feel whole again."

This comforts me a little. Jason is a counselor, so I know he has walked with many people through their grief.

I sigh and nod. I know he is right. It doesn't *feel* that way right now. But just because it feels like I will always be broken, doesn't mean that is true.

I think of the Psalms of lament. How there are pages and pages of the Psalmist complaining to God about how bad things are. How the Psalmist asks God why they have been abandoned. Are they being punished? Does God not love them anymore? Will it be this bad forever?

These Psalms are my favorite because someone out there has been as dramatic as me. Someone has pitched fit after fit to God about their life circumstances. And then—

There is always a turn, once the writer has gotten their feelings out. They remember that this is God—the same God who created the earth and brought the Israelites out of Egypt and back from exile in Babylon. This is the God who loves, who is faithful.

Reading these Psalms helps me remember that the bad parts won't last forever. They may last longer than I wish. But God will be faithful to heal, to save, to love.

I don't know what my fifty-first year will bring. I don't know how God is going to take these pieces and mend them back together into a new Dena. But I am trying to trust that I will be made new. I will not feel broken forever.

I wash my face and put on some more lip gloss. It's almost time for us to leave for dinner. I apologize to Jason for the unkind things I said while I was mad. I pick up my cardigan and my bag. I don't know how much fun dinner will be, but I will try. That has been my motto this past year, and I suspect it will be for the next one as well.

I will try to put one foot in front of the other each day. Try to do the best I can under the circumstances. Try to remember it will get better. Some days it goes great; some days, not so much. But I have to help participate in my own healing. Mending one piece at a time.

CHAPTER 27

Psalm 145

1 I will extol you, my God and King,
and bless your name forever and ever.
2 Every day I will bless you
and praise your name forever and ever.
3 Great is the Lord and greatly to be praised;
his greatness is unsearchable.

4 One generation shall extol your works to another
and shall declare your mighty acts.
5 They will recount the glorious splendor of your majesty,
and on your wondrous works I will meditate.
6 They will proclaim the might of your awesome deeds,
and I will declare your greatness.
7 They shall celebrate the fame of your abundant goodness
and shall sing aloud of your righteousness.

8 The LORD is gracious and merciful,
slow to anger and abounding in steadfast love.
9 The LORD is good to all,
and his compassion is over all that he has made.

10 All your works shall give thanks to you, O LORD,
and all your faithful shall bless you.
11 They shall speak of the glory of your kingdom
and tell of your power,
12 to make known to all people your mighty deeds
and the glorious splendor of your kingdom.
13 Your kingdom is an everlasting kingdom,
and your dominion endures throughout all generations.

The LORD is faithful in all his words
and gracious in all his deeds.
14 The LORD upholds all who are falling
and raises up all who are bowed down.
15 The eyes of all look to you,
and you give them their food in due season.
16 You open your hand,
satisfying the desire of every living thing.
17 The LORD is just in all his ways
and kind in all his doings.
18 The LORD is near to all who call on him,
to all who call on him in truth.
19 He fulfills the desire of all who fear him;
he also hears their cry and saves them.
20 The LORD watches over all who love him,
but all the wicked he will destroy.

21 My mouth will speak the praise of the LORD,
and all flesh will bless his holy name forever and ever.

MIGHT HAVE BEEN

I PICK UP A figurine of a castle to see how much it costs. The answer is too much. "Mom, what do you think of this little sheep? You think my roommate would like it?" Libby asks. I smile and nod. Since it is one of our last days in Scotland, Libby and I are souvenir shopping on the Royal Mile after touring Edinburgh Castle. I thought it would be an easy and affordable place to pick up some gifts, but the sheer number of trinkets is overwhelming me.

We pay for the sheep and head back onto the crowded cobbled street, making our way slowly down the hill away from the castle towards Holyrood Palace. I see a shop selling tweed purses and tartan scarves. "Can we pop in there real quick?" I ask. I eye a nice wrap in the Douglas tartan. It is beautiful, but I bought a lavender and green wrap on the Isle of Skye that reminded me of the colors of the countryside. And I have two Douglas tartan wool scarves in my closet at home. How much wool does a Georgia girl need?

Bagpipes greet us back on the street. A small crowd of people listen to a piper play "Scotland the Brave." Maybe it's because we're at the end of our two-week journey and

I've already heard this song countless times, but I have no desire to linger. "Don't they know another song?" Libby asks. "And why is it always American tourists walking around in kilts?"

I shake my head. "I don't know, honey. I think they're just looking for something they wish they had."

Honestly, I can relate. On this trip, I keep wondering what my life might have been like if my ancestors had stayed in Scotland—what would it be like to belong to a place people feel so proud of. Growing up in the American South, my feelings about my homeland have always been complicated.

I love some of our traditions. Growing up, we ate dinner every week after church at my grandmother's house, crowding around her table filled with fried chicken and all the fixings. I sat under the Friday night lights cheering the home team and watched SEC football in the den on Saturdays. Some things make me feel rooted and proud as a Southerner.

And other things don't. Growing up in the seventies and eighties, I was one of the first generations to experience fully integrated schools from kindergarten onwards. Let's just say things were still a bit rocky. As a child, it was confusing to realize not everyone approved of your new classroom bestie and the cool beads in her braided hair. Especially if you got a crush on a person of another race.

The older I became, the more conflicted I was to be from the South. I often wished my home state was different. That my life there was different.

And if I am truly honest, these feelings were about more than systemic racism alone. One of the aspects of grief is that we often grieve the way we wish things had been. We wish our relationship with our dying loved one had been better. That they had been better to us, that we had been better to them.

This was true with my parents and me. I always knew they loved me, but I sometimes wished they could have shown it differently. My Dad was always very protective of me and had a definite plan for my life: I would go to college—preferably one close by and as cheap as possible—earn a degree, and get a practical, useful job.

I was on board with part of this plan. I wanted to pursue both a bachelor's and a master's degree. But when I changed my career path to ministry and wanted to attend a seminary several states away, he grew confused. What happened to close and practical?

Getting married to my husband at a young age cut off our conflict to some degree, but my dad's confusion continued. Even when I self-published my first book, a lovely Advent devotional, his main comment was that it would have been more practical to publish a book that could be read year-round. Who might I have been if I had a Dad who supported me as I spread my wings? Would I have felt as obligated to move back to Georgia and do something that would make him proud?

Mom and I had our own issues. Looking back, many of these were issues she had with herself that she projected onto me. We didn't have a visit when she did not mention my weight, either in positive or negative terms. If my weight was not at an approved level, she would offer to pay for a weight loss program or gym membership. In fact, later one of the ways I knew she was developing dementia was when she stopped making comments about my weight. What would it have been like to have a mother who thought I was beautiful no matter what the scale said? Would I be more confident, less anxious?

Many of us have regrets about our relationships with loved ones. We carry thoughts about what might have been. If only things could have been this way, I would have been happier. If only they could have loved me unconditionally, I would be a better person. When we grieve a parent who has died, we often grieve not only who they were, but who we wish they could have been for us. Or we grieve the reconciliation and closure we wish we had experienced.

After I talked about these issues with my spiritual director, she gave me an exercise to do. She encouraged me to pray back over my family tree—for forgiveness and healing for my parents, grandparents, and great-grandparents, even as they rest in the heavenly realm. She hoped that this practice would help me offer forgiveness to my ancestors and find closure.

She then encouraged me to pray forward on my family tree, starting with myself. She suggested I pray for healing and blessing over my life, my children's lives, and the lives of any future grandchildren—that we would know God's works, God's great love and forgiveness, and be set free from any generational wounds. That in God, we would be free.

As I prayed back over my family and then prayed forward, I was humbled by the enormity of God's grace. How God can hold the mass of mortals, faulty and failing, and forgive us. How God holds us in love even when we cannot love ourselves. This sea of grace held me as I forgave my parents for their frailty. We are but grass, after all. I continued to pray for the ability to pass a portion of God's love and grace onto my children. I prayed any mistakes I made would be covered by God's compassionate care.

An amazing thing happens when we realize the depth of God's mercy and compassion for us. We can offer some of that compassion to others, even strangers on the street. As I watch the kilted American clap to the piper's tune, I pray they would know God's love. That they would find rest for their restless hearts in the compassionate arms of their Savior.

After all, our earthly homes are only temporary. One day we will leave this complicated earth and find our true home in heaven. What a song they must play on the streets there!

CHAPTER 28

Psalm 137

1 By the rivers of Babylon—
there we sat down, and there we wept
when we remembered Zion.
2 On the willows there
we hung up our harps.
3 For there our captors
asked us for songs,
and our tormentors asked for mirth, saying,
"Sing us one of the songs of Zion!"

4 How could we sing the LORD's song
in a foreign land?
5 If I forget you, O Jerusalem,
let my right hand wither!
6 Let my tongue cling to the roof of my mouth,
if I do not remember you,
if I do not set Jerusalem
above my highest joy.

7 Remember, O LORD, against the Edomites
the day of Jerusalem's fall,

how they said, "Tear it down! Tear it down!
Down to its foundations!"
8 O daughter Babylon, you devastator!
Happy shall they be who pay you back
what you have done to us!
9 Happy shall they be who take your little ones
and dash them against the rock!

NO SONG

AS WE WALK through the wooden doors, a great stone sanctuary opens up before us. The flying buttresses lift my eyes to the gold cross hanging over the altar area. We left ahead of schedule to get to St Mary's Episcopal—partly because we didn't know if we would get lost, and partly because we are always glad to arrive at a cathedral early. More time for us to look around and admire the beauty of this space dedicated to God's glory.

I am immediately drawn towards the altar. The architecture is Gothic, even though the church was not built until the 1800s: an altar rail, raised pulpit, choir seating on the sides behind, and at the back, a high altar crowned with stained glass. I wonder what it would be like to stand in the elevated pulpit and read the Word of God to the congregation.

The choir is in their pews, practicing for the service, and their voices drift through the sanctuary as we stand listening. St Mary's offers an Evensong service four evenings a week as a part of their ministry in the city. I remember reading about their music program online while researching churches to visit while in Scotland. This church takes choral worship leadership seriously—a quality that feels like music to our family's ears.

As the time nears for the service to begin, Jason and the kids slip into one of the front pews while I head to the back of the nave for our worship bulletins. Once seated, I scan the service to see what hymns we'll be singing—I do love my hymns. Finally, the priest welcomes those gathered.

As she explains what is to come, I realize for the first time that this is a choral Evensong—the choir will sing all the worship music alone. We will not be joining in. I suppose this makes sense in a church offering a service open to tourists unfamiliar with Episcopalian worship. But we are familiar. My kids have grown up singing harmony on hymns and chanting Psalms, and I've attended congregational Evensongs where everyone sang the entire service together. I am almost insulted we won't be able to lift our voices with the choir.

But then I take a deep breath and remember that this service is a gift. The choir is offering worship on our behalf. I close my eyes and listen as they begin to lift us in song.

As I ride upon their voices, I remember the last time I was sung for in worship. It was the first Sunday I went to church after my dad died. I knew I wanted to return to services. Sitting at home and crying on Sundays would only get me so far. But when the organ cued the processional hymn, I could make no sound. Grief had struck me dumb. I don't know if my body knew that if I sang, I would sob, or if I simply lost the ability to lift my voice in song.

As Psalm 137 says, "How can we sing the songs of the LORD while in a foreign land? If I forget you, Jerusalem, may my right hand forget its skill. May my tongue cling to the roof of my mouth if I do not remember you." My tongue clung to the roof of my mouth with grief. I couldn't even form the words. I stood still while the rest of my congregation carried the song for me.

This went on for weeks. Sometimes I could chant a Psalm or sing the Alleluia, but hymn singing eluded me. My soul knew I was too sad and too lost in grief to give praise. During that time, I leaned on my church community. I've heard it said that we say the Creeds together because when one member of the body doubts, the others can pray the creed for them until their faith returns. That became true for me with the hymns. If I could not praise God, my church family praised for me. They held me in my grief and brought my sad self to the feet of God's throne.

Over time, I regained the ability to sing in church. Not every hymn every week—but I could sing. After my fast from singing, joining my voice with the rest of our congregation felt sweeter than ever. Not because my voice was the best one, far from it, but because together we lift each other up to the altar of God.

Back at the cathedral, I try to focus less on how good the choir is (though they are so good) and more on the experience of being wrapped in vocal praise. I allow myself to rise and fall with their melodies and find companionship in their harmonies. Certain words from the songs pierce my soul.

After about half an hour, the service ends. The choir packs up and leaves the altar as if it is just another day. But I know I have experienced something special. I have not been sung to, I have been sung for. Walking out into the evening streets, I give thanks to God that our church is a communion of saints who hold each other in prayer and in song. And in this way, we never walk alone.

CHAPTER 29

Psalm 8

1 O LORD, our Sovereign,
how majestic is your name in all the earth!

You have set your glory above the heavens.
2 Out of the mouths of babes and infants
you have founded a bulwark because of your foes,
to silence the enemy and the avenger.

3 When I look at your heavens, the work of your fingers,
the moon and the stars that you have established;
4 what are humans that you are mindful of them,
mortals that you care for them?

5 Yet you have made them a little lower than God
and crowned them with glory and honor.
6 You have given them dominion over
the works of your hands;
you have put all things under their feet,
7 all sheep and oxen,
and also the beasts of the field,
8 the birds of the air, and the fish of the sea,

whatever passes along the paths of the seas.

9 O LORD, our Sovereign,
how majestic is your name in all the earth!

TOPS OFF

I FOLLOW MY DAUGHTER across the multi-lane crosswalk towards Edinburgh's Grassmarket district. "Hey Mom, let's head over to this park and take pictures. It looks really pretty." I tuck the packages of souvenirs we bought on Rose Street into my backpack and pull out my phone.

"Alright. It's a beautiful, blue-sky day. Let's do it. Princes Street Gardens looks big—where do you want to start?"

We walk down a pathway towards some pink flowering bushes to take birthday photos. We hadn't planned to spend Libby's twenty-first birthday in Scotland, but when our trip stretched past that day, she didn't complain.

Libby smooths her dress as she settles into the grass. "Okay, can you see the flowers if I sit here? Oh gosh, do you think those people are watching us?"

I glance back at the groups of people sprawled across the newly green lawn. "No, I don't think they are worried about you. They seem pretty content to lie on their blankets and soak up the sun. Funny how it is seventy degrees and everyone's in shorts and short sleeves, isn't it?" This weather would still be considered cool back home.

After our photo shoot, we wind through the rest of the park toward Grassmarket. Libby guides us along cobbled streets and narrow alleyways to the meeting spot for our afternoon food tour. When we greet our tour guide, he asks if we found the restaurant easily. I laugh. "Oh yeah—we cut through the park. There were so many people out today. I couldn't believe all the guys lying in the sun with their shirts off!"

Our guide breaks into a wide smile. "Oh, aye. Today is what we call a tops-off day—the first of the spring, in fact. The cold, cloudy days have finally given way to warm, sunny weather. We Scots have to celebrate that in style!"

"I hadn't thought about it that way, but it makes sense." I try to imagine living through a long Scottish winter. It doesn't snow much in Edinburgh, but it gets cold. And it gets dark. Soul-wearingly dark.

Though the weather in Georgia stays mild most of the winter, I know a little bit about the soul-wearingly dark part. If not in physicality, at least in spirit.

The past two winters had been hard for us. The winter of 2023 ushered in Mom's sickness and death. I knew those cold, barren days would be her last. And the winter of 2024 came down like a blanket of grief. When the dark descended that December, I felt like I would never smile again. I sat evening after evening swaddled in blankets, dogs on the sofa, feeling the empty night of loved ones lost.

Sometimes in the middle of our spiritual winters, it can seem the sun will never shine again. That we will never hear the sound of our own laugh. And then it happens. The cold wind dies down and the clouds part. The sun peeks its head out once again.

The first time I laughed after my parents died, I

remember feeling conflicted. The bubbles of joy felt like a respite amidst so many tears. Then came the guilt. How could I laugh after suffering so deep a loss? How could I disrespect Mom and Dad's deaths by not feeling sad? Soon enough, the sadness returned.

The next time the laughter came, I recognized it for what it was: a welcome break in a long, dark winter of heavy grief. I soaked it up this time, not knowing when it would come again.

Like a resident of northern Europe feeling the sun, I soon learned to soak up any joy that arose in my life as a lifeline. I would store this joy deep within, just as my pasty ancestors stored Vitamin D.

For we cannot live without sunshine and all it brings. Nor can we live without joy and praise to God for the goodness of this world and our life in it.

We must cry out like the Psalmist, "O Lord, our Sovereign, how majestic is your name in all the earth!" We must be able to look at the glory all around us and give thanks for God's wonderful works. Even in grief. Even in sadness.

It is a funny thing about those tops-off days when the sun breaks through my grief. The more I lean into praise and gratitude on those days, the longer they last—and the more often they come. Like an injured person learning to walk again, I grow in my ability to notice the good things around me and be glad for them. In my grief, I re-learn to praise God.

But now the praise is deeper because it comes from a heart carved out with sorrow and refilled with joy.

As my family heads out along the streets of Scotland for a day of good food and drink, our laughter rings out along the stone streets. We are happy. The day is beautiful. My family is beautiful. These moments are beautiful. I give thanks to God for all these blessings and soak in my joy. Another hard day is sure to come, and when the clouds of sorrow build again, I will need this moment of sunshine to remember.

CHAPTER 30

Psalm 84

1 How lovely is your dwelling place,
O LORD of hosts!
2 My soul longs, indeed it faints,
for the courts of the LORD;
my heart and my flesh sing for joy
to the living God.

3 Even the sparrow finds a home
and the swallow a nest for herself,
where she may lay her young,
at your altars, O LORD of hosts,
my King and my God.
4 Happy are those who live in your house,
ever singing your praise.

5 Happy are those whose strength is in you,
in whose heart are the highways to Zion.
6 As they go through the valley of Baca,
they make it a place of springs;
the early rain also covers it with pools.
7 They go from strength to strength;

the God of gods will be seen in Zion.

8 O LORD God of hosts, hear my prayer;
give ear, O God of Jacob! Selah
9 Behold our shield, O God;
look on the face of your anointed.

10 For a day in your courts is better
than a thousand elsewhere.
I would rather be a doorkeeper in the house of my God
than live in the tents of wickedness.
11 For the LORD God is a sun and shield;
he bestows favor and honor.
No good thing does the LORD withhold
from those who walk uprightly.
12 O LORD of hosts,
happy is everyone who trusts in you.

CALEDONIA

I SMELL THE SPOONFUL of soup before I dare taste it. I read in all the travel blogs you have to try Cullen Skink while in Scotland, so when I saw it on the menu at the pub, I ordered it straight away. Looking at the bowl, I realize I have never tried a fish soup before. Oyster stew, shrimp chowder, and crab bisque are all favorites of mine, so I take a chance and drink down the milky broth. "Mmmm, creamy and mild." I give a thumbs up to my family seated at the booth with me.

"The steak pie is good too," my daughter affirms. It is one of our last nights in Scotland, so we are going all out, trying traditional dishes at a touristy pub known for its music. We have eaten a lot of different fare while here—amazing Indian food in Glasgow, top-notch pizza on Skye, and some of the best ravioli we have ever tasted at an inn at Fort William. We didn't want to do what the Scots call a touristy twee tour, experiencing only an idyllic image of Scottish life. Instead, we wanted to balance history with modern Scotland as it is.

But tonight, we are a little twee with our pints and old-school dishes in a pub off the Royal Mile in Edinburgh.

A cheer goes up in the front room as the musician starts another sea shanty. Everyone loves banging their beer on the table as they sing along to the familiar tune.

As we slow down over our meal, the music does too. The performer starts a wistful guitar intro I have never heard before. As he moves into the lyrics, I listen closely: "I've been telling old stories, singing songs that make me think about where I came from and that's the reason why I seem so far away today." I look at Jason, and he opens the music identifier app on his phone. He shows me the screen listing the original artist as Dougie MacLean and the song title as "Caledonia."

As the singer moves into the chorus, tears prick my eyes: "But let me tell you that I love you, that I think about you all the time. Caledonia, you're calling me, and now I'm going home."

I can't explain the lump in my throat. The song seems to capture a mix of emotions that have defined this past year—love, leaving, longing, and a wish to be reunited once again.

This sense of home is something I have been searching for over the past months—because I lost mine. The trifecta of losing my mother, my father, and my childhood home in six months was a gut punch I have not been able to recover from. Not that my home was perfect—far from it. But it was mine. My parents were mine. My childhood with them was mine. And now so much of that feels lost.

That lostness is part of what brought me to Scotland. I thought if I could see the land of my ancestors—some ancient home I had never known—I might feel reconnected somehow. In some ways, I have. In others, I have missed my parents here even more than I did in my hometown.

I think that is part of my grief. Missing and saying goodbye to something I will never have on this earth again. I will never have my home with my parents living in it in my lifetime. That part of me is gone.

But it does not mean it will be forgotten.

I will hold my parents in my heart every day. They are part of me and always will be. I see them in the mirror, in the shape of my biological son, and in the mannerisms of my adopted daughter. They are imprinted on my life in a way that cannot be removed.

The chorus of the song rings out again, "But let me tell you that I love you, that I think about you all the time. Caledonia, you're calling me, and now I'm going home." I wonder what home means for me now. Is it the house I live in with my husband each day? This place we welcome our kids back to when they are home from college. Is it the county I have spent most of my life in and find my way through by heart?

Or is it something more? I have always resonated with the idea of being homesick for heaven. Somehow, we know we are not fully citizens of Earth, and heaven is our true home. To some degree, we will also be restless until we rest in peace in God's home.

It feels like that longing has been cranked up a few notches since my parents went to their eternal home. I am now here without them, missing them and my dwelling place with God both.

But this homesickness is not complete nor will it last forever. I have always believed in thin places, spots where the veil between heaven and earth gets thin and we can feel a bit of God's presence and feel a bit of God's glory. I feel this way at my favorite retreat center, when visiting the North Georgia mountains, and now here in Scotland. This connection with heaven makes the longing hurt less for a while.

And when the longing does flare up, I remind myself this is a temporary problem. One day I will dwell in God's house. Though that day seems far away now, in the scope of eternity, it is only a heartbeat away. These earthly struggles will pale in comparison to the joy and fulfillment of being reunited with my parents, friends, and God.

This life on earth will one day pass away and I will dwell in the courts of the LORD. Then all these tears will be wiped away and my grief will be a faint memory. Until then, I live in hope with the God who comforts me in the meantime and one day will make all things new.

ACKNOWLEDGEMENTS

No one ever truly writes a book alone. I am so thankful for everyone who inspired and supported me during the creation of this book.

Thanks to my Page 24 Word Weavers writing group. You all held me gently and cheered heartily as I wrote this book with you. Love to you all. I am most grateful to early readers Kirsten, Debbie, Jenn, Nikki, and Jason. Your time, comments, and encouragement mean so much.

Thanks and more thanks to my editor Alynda. You are an editing genius! Thank you for pushing me to be my best and for loving the em dash even more than me. Also thank you to Joe for bringing my cover idea to life.

I am endlessly grateful for my dear family: Jason, Libby, and Eli. Thanks for taking the great Scotland pilgrimage with me and for walking alongside me during such a hard time in all of our lives. I love you all more than you could know.

And to Mom and Dad. I felt you nearby as I was writing these words and remembering our life together. Thanks for making me who I am and loving me always. As Song of Solomon says, "Set me as a seal upon your heart, as a seal upon your arm, for love is strong as death."

ABOUT THE AUTHOR

Dena Douglas Hobbs, MDiv, is a campus minister for the Episcopal and Lutheran denominations. She is the co-author of *When Anxiety Strikes: Help and Hope for Managing Your Storm* and the author of *Lighten the Darkness: An Advent Journey Through Hope*. You can follow her writing at *Stubborn Grace by Dena Douglas Hobbs* on Substack.

www.ingramcontent.com/pod-product-compliance
Lightning Source LLC
Jackson TN
JSHW080924260226
98596JS00012B/66
* 9 7 9 8 9 9 4 7 6 1 8 0 9 *